S0-AGI-177

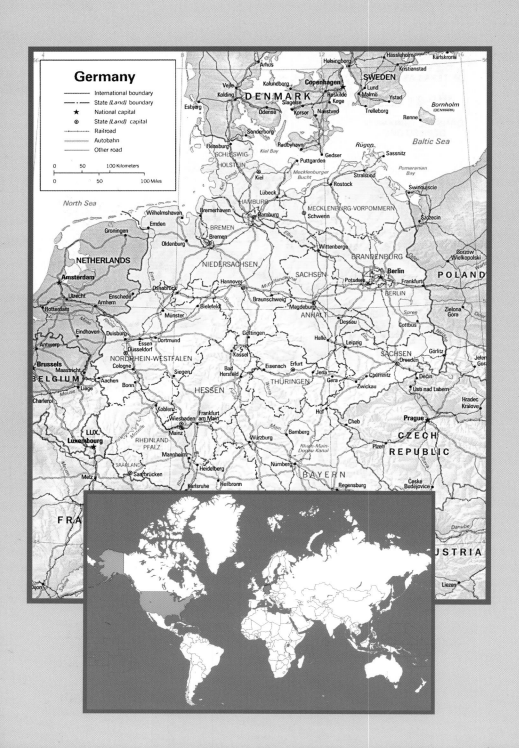

Germany

- International boundary
- State *(Land)* boundary
- ★ National capital
- ⊛ State *(Land)* capital
- Railroad
- Autobahn
- Other road

0   50   100 Kilometers

0   50   100 Miles

North Sea

Baltic Sea

DENMARK

Århus
Vejle
Kolding
Esbjerg
Kalundborg
Slagelse
Odense
Korsør
Sønderborg
Copenhagen
Roskilde
Køge
Næstved
Helsingborg
Hässleholm
Kärlskrona
Kristianstad

SWEDEN

Lund
Malmö
Ystad
Trelleborg
Rønne
Bornholm
(DENMARK)

Flensburg
Kiel Bay
Rødbyhavn
Gedser
Puttgarden
Sassnitz
Rügen

SCHLESWIG-HOLSTEIN
Kiel
Mecklenburger Bucht
Rostock
Stralsund
Pomeranian Bay
Swinoujście

Wilhelmshaven
Emden
Bremerhaven
HAMBURG
Hamburg
Schwerin
MECKLENBURG-VORPOMMERN
Szczecin

Groningen
Oldenburg
BREMEN
Bremen
Wittenberge
BRANDENBURG
Gorzów
Wielkopolski

NETHERLANDS
Amsterdam
Utrecht
Enschede
Arnhem
Osnabrück
Hannover
NIEDERSACHSEN
SACHSEN-
Potsdam
Berlin
BERLIN
Frankfurt
POLAND

Rotterdam
Eindhoven
Duisburg
Essen
Düsseldorf
Dortmund
Münster
Bielefeld
Braunschweig
Magdeburg
ANHALT
Dessau
Cottbus
Zielona
Góra

Antwerp
Brussels
Maastricht
Liège
NORDRHEIN-WESTFALEN
Cologne
Aachen
Bonn
Siegen
Göttingen
Halle
Leipzig
SACHSEN
Dresden
Görlitz
Jelen
Gora

BELGIUM
Charleroi
Kassel
Bad
Hersfeld
Eisenach
Erfurt
Jena
Gera
Chemnitz
Děčín
Ústí nad Labem
Hradec
Králové

HESSEN
THÜRINGEN
Zwickau
Hof
Cheb
Prague

Koblenz
Frankfurt
am Main
Wiesbaden
Mainz
Würzburg
Bamberg
Plzen
CZECH
REPUBLIC

LUX.
Luxembourg
RHEINLAND-
PFALZ
Mannheim
Heidelberg
Nürnberg
České
Budějovice

Metz
SAARLAND
Saarbrücken
Karlsruhe
Heilbronn
BAYERN
Regensburg

FRA

Dijon

USTRIA

Liezen

Danube

IMMIGRANTS IN AMERICA

German
AMERICANS

Liz Sonneborn

CHELSEA HOUSE
PUBLISHERS
A Haights Cross Communications Company

Philadelphia

Frontispiece: Map of Germany with world map inset. German immigrants endured a long and harsh journey across the Atlantic Ocean for a new and better life.

CHELSEA HOUSE PUBLISHERS

VP, NEW PRODUCT DEVELOPMENT Sally Cheney
DIRECTOR OF PRODUCTION Kim Shinners
CREATIVE MANAGER Takeshi Takahashi
MANUFACTURING MANAGER Diann Grasse

Staff for GERMAN AMERICANS

ASSISTANT EDITOR Kate Sullivan
PRODUCTION EDITOR Jaimie Winkler
PICTURE RESEARCHER Pat Holl
SERIES DESIGNER Takeshi Takahashi
COVER DESIGNER Takeshi Takahashi
LAYOUT 21st Century Publishing and Communications, Inc.

A Haights Cross Communications ✦ Company

http://www.chelseahouse.com

First Printing

1 3 5 7 9 8 6 4 2

Library of Congress Cataloging-in-Publication Data

Sonneborn, Liz.
    German Americans / Liz Sonneborn.
        p. cm. — (Immigrants in America)
Includes bibliographical references.
    ISBN 0-7910-7127-8HC   07910-7512-5PB
    1. German Americans—Juvenile literature. 2. German Americans—History—
Juvenile literature. [1. German Americans. 2. Immigrants.] I. Title. II. Series:
Immigrants in America (Chelsea House Publishers)
E184.G3 S73 2002
973'.0431—dc21
                                                          2002015906

CONTENTS

A NATION OF NATIONS

Daniel Patrick Moynihan

The Constitution of the United States begins: "We the People of the United States . . ." Yet, as we know, the United States was not then and is not now made up of a single group. It is made up of many peoples. Immigrants and bondsmen from Europe, Asia, the Pacific Islands, Africa, and Central and South America came here or were brought here, and still they come. They forged one nation and made it their own. More than 100 years ago, Walt Whitman expressed this great central fact of America: "Here is not merely a nation, but a teeming Nation of nations."

Although the ingenuity and acts of courage of these immigrants, our ancestors, shaped the North American way of life, we sometimes take their contributions for granted. This fine series, IMMIGRANTS IN AMERICA, examines the experiences and contributions of different immigrant groups and how these contributions determined the future of the United States and Canada.

Immigrants did not abandon their ethnic traditions when they reached the shores of North America. Each ethnic group had its own customs and traditions, and each brought different experiences, accomplishments, skills, values, styles of dress, and tastes in food that lingered long after its arrival. Yet this profusion of differences created a bond among immigrants. Ethnic foods, for example, sometimes became "typically" American, such as frankfurters, pizzas, and tacos.

The United States and Canada are unusual in this respect. Whereas religious and ethnic differences have sparked intolerance throughout the rest of the world, North Americans have struggled to learn how to respect each other's differences and live in harmony.

Our two countries are hardly the only two in which different groups must learn to live together. There is no nation of significant size anywhere in the world that would not be classified as multiethnic. But only in North America are there so *many* different groups, most of them living cheek by jowl with one another.

This is not easy. Look around the world. And it has not always been easy for us. Witness the exclusion of Chinese immigrants, and for practical purposes the Japanese also, in the late nineteenth century. But by the late twentieth century, Chinese and Japanese Americans were the most successful of all the groups recorded by the census. We have had prejudice aplenty, but it has been resisted and recurrently overcome.

The remarkable ability of Americans to live together as one people was seriously threatened by the issue of slavery. Thousands of settlers from the British Isles had arrived in the colonies as indentured servants, agreeing to work for a specified number of years on farms or as apprentices in return for passage to America and room and board. When the first Africans arrived in the then-British colonies during the seventeenth century, some colonists thought that they, too, should be treated as indentured servants. Eventually, the question of whether the Africans should be treated as indentured, like the English, or as slaves who could be owned for life, was considered in a Maryland court. The court's calamitous decree held that blacks were slaves bound to a lifelong servitude, and so also were their children. America went through a time of moral examination and civil war before African slaves and their descendants were finally freed. The principle that all people are created equal had faced its greatest challenge and it survived.

Yet the court ruling that set blacks apart from other races fanned flames of discrimination that burned long after slavery was abolished—and that still flicker today. Indeed, it was about the time of the American Civil War that European theories of evolution were turned to the service of ranking different peoples by their presumed distance from our apelike ancestors!

When the Irish flooded American cities to escape the famine in Ireland, the cartoonists caricatured the typical "Paddy" (a common term for Irish immigrants) as an apelike creature with jutting jaw and sloping forehead.

By the twentieth century, racism and ethnic prejudice had given rise to virulent theories of a Northern European master race. When Adolf Hitler came to power in Germany in 1933, he popularized the notion of an Aryan race. Only a man of the deepest ignorance and evil could have done this. *Aryan* is a Sanskrit word taken from the ancient language of the civilizations that inhabited the Indus Valley, which now includes Pakistan and much of Northern India. The term "Aryan," which means "noble," was first used by the eminent German linguist Max Müller to denote the Indo-European family of languages. Müller was horrified that anyone could think of it in terms of a race of blond-haired, blue-eyed Teutons. But the Nazis embraced the notion of a master race. Anyone with darker and heavier features was considered inferior. Buttressed by these theories, the German Nazi state from 1933 to 1945 set out to destroy European Jews, along with Poles, Gypsies, Russians, and other groups considered inferior. They nearly succeeded. Millions of these people were murdered.

The tragedies brought on by ethnic and racial intolerance throughout the world demonstrate the importance of North America's efforts to create a society free of prejudice and inequality.

A relatively recent example of the New World's desire to resolve ethnic friction nonviolently is the solution that the Canadians found to a conflict between two ethnic groups. A long-standing dispute as to whether Canadian culture was properly English or properly French resurfaced in the mid-1960s, dividing the peoples of the French-speaking Province of Quebec from those of the English-speaking provinces. Relations grew tense, then bitter, then violent. The Royal Commission on Bilingualism and Biculturalism was established to study the growing crisis and to propose measures to ease the tensions. As a result of the commission's recommendations, all official documents and statements from the national government's capital at Ottawa are now issued in both French and English, and bilingual education is encouraged. But the commissioners recorded that there were many other groups as well.

Toward the end of the nineteenth century in the United States, public figures such as Theodore Roosevelt began speaking about "Americanism," deploring "hyphenated Americans" as persons only partly assimilated—later it would be said insufficiently loyal—to their adopted country. Ethnicity was seen by many as a threat to national cohesion, and even to national security. During World War I, referring to German Americans, Roosevelt would speak of "the Hun within." During World War II, immigrant Germans and Italians were classified as "enemy aliens," and Japanese Americans were settled in detention camps. With time, however, we became more accepting as ethnicity emerged as a *form* of Americanism, celebrated in the annual Columbus Day and Steuben Day parades, the West Indian parade, the Pakistani parade, and in New York City the venerable St. Patrick's Day parade, which dates back before the American Revolution.

In time, the Bureau of the Census took note. In 1980, for the first time, the census questionnaire asked, "What is this person's ancestry?" In parentheses, it stated: "For example: Afro-American, English, French, German" and so on through a list of 16 possibilities, followed by "etc." The results were a bit misleading. Remember, it was a new question. Census officials now speculate that because the first European group listed was English, many respondents simply stopped there. The result was an "overcount." By 2000, however, the bureau was getting better.

The 2000 census also asked people to identify their ancestry. More than 80 percent chose one or more groups from a list of 89 different groups. Most people "specified," as the census states, a "single ancestry," but almost a quarter cited "multiple ancestry." So which is it: are we a melting pot or a "Nation of nations"? The answer is both. Americans share a common citizenship, which is the most important fact of our civic life. But most also feel part of one group or another, especially recent arrivals.

Of which there are many indeed! Since 1970 more than 26 million immigrants have entered the United States; most immigrants have entered legally, but of late not all. For the longest time, anyone could enter. Under the Constitution, drawn up in 1797, even the trade in African slaves was protected for 20 years—a hideous practice, but well established in Southern states. In time, however, hostility toward newcomers appeared, notably tinged with racial fears. In 1882 an act of U.S. Congress excluded further Chinese immigration, responding to pressure from Californians anxious about "cheap labor." Next there was agitation to exclude Japanese, which only ended when the Japanese government, in what was termed a "Gentleman's Agreement," consented to withhold passports from Japanese emigrants. Restrictions on Asians continued until 1965.

Indeed, at the end of the nineteenth century there was much talk about the "Anglo-Saxon race" and its many virtues. The United States had reached an informal alliance with Great Britain, and we were setting up an empire of our own that included the Philippines, Cuba, Puerto Rico, and Hawaii. Weren't we different from those "others"? Not exactly. Migration has been going on across the world from the beginning of time and there is no such thing as a pure race. The humorist Finley Peter Dunne wrote: "An Anglo-Saxon…is a German that's forgot who was his parents." Indeed, following the departure of the Romans from Britain in the year A.D. 410, Germanic tribes, including Saxons from northern Germany and Anglos from southern Denmark, migrated into the British Isles. In time they defined what we now call Britain, driving the Celts to Wales and Ireland, with an essentially Celtic Scotland to the north.

Thus immigrants from the British Isles, approximately a third of the present day population of the United States, were already a heterogeneous group. Perhaps even more importantly, they belonged to many different religious denominations including the Puritan, Congregational, Episcopalian, Quaker, and Catholic churches, and even a small community of Sephardic Jews from Brazil! No group made up a majority; religious toleration came about largely because there seemed to be no alternative.

American immigration policy developed in much this way. Though completely open at the beginning, over time, efforts were made to limit the influx of certain immigrant groups, in the manner of the exclusion of Asians in the late nineteenth century and the Southern Europeans by the early twentieth century. By the 1960s, however, America was already too diverse to pretend otherwise, and immigration was opened to all nations.

The people of North America are the descendants of one of the greatest migrations in history. And that migration is not over. Koreans, Vietnamese, Mexicans, Nicaraguans, Pakistanis, Indians, Arabs, and many others are heading for the shores of North America in large numbers. This mix of cultures shapes every aspect of our lives. To understand ourselves, we must know something about our diverse ethnic ancestry. Nothing so defines the North American nations as the motto on the Great Seal of the United States: *E Pluribus Unum*—Out of Many, One. ■

1

THE GERMANS IN AMERICA

Our first and greatest debt to the Germans is for their help in developing our country. It is said of the common German laborer that the minute he lands he is worth to the country fully one thousand dollars. Multiply this figure by the hundreds of thousands who have come over, and it is easy to see how valuable this class alone has been to us.

—"The German and the German-American,"
***The Atlantic Monthly*, November 1896**

The more than seven million Germans that who immigrated to the United States over the past three centuries have helped shape the nation. The influence of German Americans on American society and culture has been so great that it is difficult to imagine what the United States would be like today without the benefit of German immigration. As the nineteenth-century German-American author Konrad Krez once wrote, "Ever wonder

Perhaps the most commonly recognized cultural element that has followed German immigrants to America is the Oktoberfest—a yearly celebration of food and drink that can be found in nearly every region where German immigrants settled.

then, what kind of land, 'twould be if ne'er a German came!"

The German Americans are unique among American ethnic groups in several ways. The most obvious is their sheer number. More than one-fourth of all Americans identify themselves as having German ancestry, making German Americans the largest ethnic group in the United States.

GERMAN-AMERICAN COMMUNITIES

The virtual invisibility of German-American culture is a relatively new phenomenon. For much of the eighteenth and nineteenth centuries, German-American communities dotted the country, with the highest concentrations in the Midwest and the Northeast. Nearly all important cities in these areas had a Little Germany—a neighborhood in which German Americans lived and gathered to socialize. These neighborhoods featured restaurants, food shops, theaters, and music halls with a distinctively German flavor. By founding these establishments, German Americans tried to recreate the atmosphere of their homeland in their new surroundings.

During this early period of German immigration, German Americans were fiercely proud of their heritage. In much of the country, they earned a reputation for their hard work, thriftiness, and respect for authority. As a consequence, Germans were more welcome in the United States than perhaps any other group of European immigrants. Many territories and states actively courted German immigrants, hoping to increase their population with these model citizens.

Ironically, German Americans have been so successful blending into the mainstream population that they are now nearly invisible. Most Americans—even those with German ancestry—would be hard-pressed to identify many customs as being German American. The only well-known elements of German-American culture are those associated with Oktoberfest and similar festivals in which Americans come together to enjoy German food, drink, and music.

REASONS FOR EMIGRATING

Despite the generalizations that arose around German Americans, German immigrants were a diverse group. They chose to emigrate for a wide variety of reasons. Some left Germany to escape religious intolerance. Others emigrated because they opposed the governments of the small states that once made up Germany. Still others ventured from the old country to seek their fortune in the United States, knowing that in America they had a far better chance of improving their financial lot.

GERMAN INFLUENCE ON AMERICAN LIFE

The diversity of the German immigrant population was in large part responsible for their enormous influence on

The Amish

The rich farmlands of Lancaster County in southeastern Pennsylvania are home to the Old Order Amish. Descended from eighteenth-century German and Swiss immigrants, their way of life has barely changed for hundreds of years.

In 1693, the Amish religious sect was formed by a Swiss bishop named Jacob Amman. Three decades later, the Amish began immigrating to Pennsylvania, the American colony distinguished for its religious tolerance. Over time, some Amish migrated to nearby states, but the most conservative remained in Lancaster County. Known as the Old Order Amish since the mid-nineteenth century, they now number about 18,000.

The Amish of Lancaster County believe that God wants them to live separately from the rest of the world. Valuing humility and self-sufficiency, they have rejected many modern conveniences. They do not own cars, preferring instead to travel in horse-drawn buggies. They also refuse to use electricity, telephones, radios, or televisions.

The Old Order Amish are guided by the Ordnung, an unwritten set of rules that govern their behavior in public and in private. They strive to keep their lives as simple as possible, concentrating their time and energy on worshipping God and working at family-owned farms and businesses. Their code of self-restraint even dictates their physical appearance. Men dress in dark colored suits. Their coats and jackets do not have lapels or buttons, which the Amish regard as frivolous decorations. Women wear solid-colored dresses with long sleeves and skirts that extend nearly to their ankles. On her wedding day, an Amish bride wears a special dress, usually made from blue or purple cloth.

From a young age, children are taught about the Amish way of life by their parents and the community. The children also attend private schools through the eighth grade run by the Amish. There, they learn English so they can speak with outsiders. In their own homes, however, they still speak a dialect of German.

The Amish often do business with people outside their community. Some even sell goods to tourists who come to Lancaster County to watch the Amish go about their old-fashioned daily routines. The Amish, though, are largely content to keep to themselves in order to preserve their treasured way of life.

American life. The Germans who came to the United States included tradesmen, artisans, merchants, farmers, teachers, writers, musicians, artists, and businessmen. It is not surprising that German Americans had a hand in developing nearly every field of activity—from agriculture to business to science to the arts. By offering America their talent and labor, German

German Immigration in Numbers

German Immigration to the United States, 1821–2000. Courtesy of the United States Immigration and Naturalization Service.

Decade	Number of Immigrants
1821–1830	6,761
1831–1840	152,454
1841–1850	434,626
1851–1860	951,667
1861–1870	787,468
1871–1880	718,182
1881–1890	1,452,970
1891–1900	505,152
1901–1910	341,498
1911–1920	143,945
1921–1930	412,202
1931–1940	114,058
1941–1950	226,578
1951–1960	477,765
1961–1970	190,796
1971–1980	74,414
1981–1990	91,961
1991–2000	92,606
TOTAL	7,176,071

Many of the Germans who immigrated to the United States were craftsmen and farmers. Applying their skills and labor in the fields of their new homeland, they quickly established thriving communities throughout the Northeast and Midwest.

Americans played a significant role in the emergence of the United States as a world power in the late nineteenth and early twentieth centuries.

HOSTILITY TOWARD GERMANS IN AMERICA

After long enjoying the status as America's most desirable immigrant group, German Americans suffered a sudden and severe blow when the United States entered World War I in 1917. With America's decision to engage in this European conflict, Germany became an enemy of the United States. In the blink of an eye, Americans grew suspicious of all things German—including German Americans. The American people and their governments tried to wipe out all German

German-American communities have retained a strong sense of their European heritage, as shown by this signpost in New Ulm, Minnesota. The signpost uses German words to point to such nearby locations as the *Bahnhöf* (train station) and such distant German cities as *München* (Munich).

influences in American life. In addition, they threatened and harassed any German Americans who were deemed too sympathetic to the German cause. Seeing the intensity of these anti-German sentiments, many German Americans became hesitant to talk about their heritage or their love of the old country.

After the war, Americans' ill will toward Germany and Germans started to fade. But by the 1930s, it was reignited after Nazi leader Adolf Hitler became the chancellor of Germany. In 1941, the United States again declared war against Germany, and German Americans again found their identity under attack. Although the anti-Germanism of the early 1940s was less pronounced than it had been during the World War I era, many German Americans, out of self-preservation, made the decision to hide their German roots.

BLENDING INTO AMERICAN LIFE

Because of their experiences during the two world wars, German Americans had largely lost their sense of group identity by the beginning of the twenty-first century. As German-American author Kurt Vonnegut has noted, "German-Americans [have] become (in self-defense and in embarrassment over Kaiser Wilhelm [the ruler of Germany during World War I] and then Hitler) the least tribal and most accultured segment of our white population."

Today, most Little Germanies and other distinctly German-American communities no longer exist. But German-American culture has hardly vanished. Instead, the ideas, beliefs, and products Germans brought to the United States are still embraced by Americans—so much so that they have been seamlessly woven into the fabric of American culture. Far from having disappeared from American life, German-American culture, in many ways, has become American life.

2

THE FATHERLAND

Although I have been in America for 23 years I still like to think now and then about the dear homeland where my cradle stood and where I spent a happy childhood, despite many a hardship. I am happy when I linger in thought among my dear brothers and sisters and relatives and the friends of my youth, as well as at the graves of my blessed parents, sister and relatives and then a quiet ache creeps into my heart, and how true the old saying becomes—be it ever so lovely in a foreign land, it never will be home—but then all at once all the troub es [*sic*] and hardships that a poor though honest laborer must endure pass before my eyes, and then I thank the dear Lord a thousand times that I escaped that land that can't even feed its own people.

—German-American farmer Franz Joseph Löwen,
in a letter written in 1880

Many German Americans still look on their homeland with loving memories. Small villages, like this one in Bavaria, have lent their names and influenced the architecture of many American towns.

The mixed emotions communicated by Franz Joseph Löwen were common among German immigrants who came to live in the United States. Even after many years in America, they often looked back to their homeland with loving memories. But these moments of reverie also conjured up darker remembrances of their lives in Germany—memories often colored by poverty, religious persecution, and political oppression.

German immigration, therefore, was not only the story of people seeking a new life in a new land. It was also the story of emigrants escaping hardships they faced in their beloved, yet troubled Fatherland.

LEGENDARY FIRST GERMAN IMMIGRANT

Legend holds that the first German to leave his homeland and set out for North America was a man named Tyrker. In about A.D. 1000, he accompanied the Vikings, or Norsemen, on a sea voyage from Scandinavia to the coast of a strange land. The expedition was led by Leif Ericsson, who considered Tyrker to be his foster father. While exploring the coast, Tyrker wandered away from the others. Ericsson led a search party, found Tyrker, and asked him where he had been. A Norse myth recounts Tyrker's response: "In the beginning Tyrker spoke for some time in German, rolling his eyes and grinning, and they could not understand him; but after a time he addressed them in the Northern tongue: 'I did not go much further than you, and yet I have something of novelty to relate. I have found vines and grapes.' . . . Leif gave the land a name, and called it Wineland." Today, the location of the Vikings' Wineland, or Vinland, is debated, though many scholars believe it was the coastal region of what is now Newfoundland, Canada.

THE GERMANS' ROLE
IN EUROPEAN IMMIGRATION

Centuries passed before other Europeans arrived in North America and South America. Only after the voyages of Christopher Columbus in the late fifteenth century did European explorers begin traveling to these continents. The explorers came from several European nations, including England, Spain, Portugal, and the Netherlands. German mapmakers and navigators created maps and nautical instruments that helped make these explorations possible. One

German geographer, Martin Waldseemüller, was responsible for naming the two continents "America" after Italian explorer Amerigo Vespucci. German writers and artists were also largely responsible for spreading information throughout Europe about these early voyages by publishing illustrated books about the places and peoples the explorers encountered.

A few Germans participated in these voyages. For instance, several were among the colonists who in 1607 founded Jamestown, the first permanent English settlement in the Americas. The Germans at Jamestown gained a reputation for working hard, but resisted following the orders of the English. According to Jamestown leader John Smith, three Germans became so fed up with the English that they left Jamestown to live with the Powhatan Indians.

The rulers of Germany themselves, however, played little role in financing and organizing expeditions to North America. One reason lay in the geography of Germany. Germany had only a small strip of coastal land in its northeastern corner, limiting access to the sea. During the Age of Exploration, the only way Europeans could reach the Americas was by sailing west across the Atlantic Ocean. Lacking good ports and a strong navy, German rulers could not sponsor major explorations as other European leaders could.

GERMANY'S ROOTS IN THE HOLY ROMAN EMPIRE

Germany's political situation also stifled its participation in the exploration of the Americas. At the time, the lands now known as Germany were not a unified nation. Instead, they were part of the Holy Roman Empire, a loose confederation of independent states in north-central Europe. The inhabitants of these states shared the German language, but otherwise did not consider themselves a unified ethnic group.

Among the more famous names in German history is that of Martin Luther. In 1517, Luther led a break from the Catholic Church that established Protestantism as a new branch of Christianity.

RELIGIOUS WARS

In the sixteenth century, the German states were also embroiled in a series of religious wars. The wars began in 1517 after a German monk named Martin Luther broke away from the Roman Catholic Church and established a new branch of

Christianity known as Protestantism. Sharing Luther's belief that the leaders of the Catholic Church were corrupt, many German peasants embraced his ideas. Some German rulers also converted to Lutheranism, whereas others continued to practice Catholicism. These religious differences led to bloodshed. Trying to end the fighting, Holy Roman Emperor Charles V agreed to the Peace of Augsburg of 1555. This peace established the principle of *cuius regio, eius religio*—a Latin phrase that means "whoever owns the region determines the religion." This allowed the prince or duke who controlled a German state to determine what its official religion would be.

For many Germans, this policy was devastating. Protestants and Catholics alike found themselves in states that opposed their religious beliefs, forcing them to leave their homes and move to other parts of Europe. The policy also did little to end the religious wars within the Holy Roman Empire. In 1618, Protestants in the state of Bohemia revolted against Catholic rule. Ferdinand II, the Holy Roman Emperor and a devout Catholic, sent soldiers into the region, prompting the Thirty Years' War (1618–1648). The war spread throughout much of Europe, but southwestern German states such as the Palatinate and Baden saw the worst fighting. During the conflict, about one-third of the German population died, many from starvation and epidemic disease. In the hardest hit areas, the death toll rose as high as 75 percent. Along with the loss of human life, Germans suffered greatly, since many of their villages and farms were destroyed.

GERMANS SEEK RELIGIOUS FREEDOM

When the war ended in 1648, the Holy Roman Empire was left weaker than ever. Germany was divided into about 300 separate states, none bigger than a large city. Many Germans continued to face religious oppression from the petty rulers. The most oppressed were the members of newly created sects of Protestantism, such as the Mennonites and Moravians.

In 1683, a group of 13 Mennonite families left Germany to seek religious freedom in the English colonies of North America. They had been invited to the colony of Pennsylvania by its founder, William Penn. Penn and his followers were Quakers, members of a Protestant sect established in England during the middle of the seventeenth century.

GERMANS IN PENNSYLVANIA

Led by Francis Daniel Pastorius, the German Mennonites arrived in Pennsylvania on October 6, 1683. They bought 43,000 acres outside the town of Philadelphia. The area, known as Germantown, became the first German settlement in North America. Pastorius declared that his followers' mission was "to lead a quiet, godly, and honest life in a howling wilderness." Germantown was an immediate success. Largely artisans and farmers, the Mennonites quickly built a prosperous settlement, surrounded by fields, orchards, and vineyards

GERMANS CONDEMN SLAVERY

The Germans became content with their new homeland, although they were appalled by Pennsylvania's acceptance of the practice of slavery. On April 18, 1688, the residents of Germantown sent a petition to Philadelphia. As the first formal protest against slavery drafted in North America, it asked the following question: "Pray what thing in the world can be done worse toward us if men should rob or steal us away and sell us for slaves to strange countries separating husband from their wife and children?" Seventeen years later, the Quaker leadership in Philadelphia passed a resolution condemning the slave trade.

MORE GERMAN IMMIGRATION

As word of the success of Germantown spread, other German religious groups began immigrating to the English colonies. Most went to Pennsylvania, but some settled in other

Many Protestant groups, like the Mennonites, found themselves oppressed by the Catholic rulers of Germany's small city-states. Seeking religious tolerance, many left their homeland and established churches like this one in Germantown, Pennsylvania (now a Philadelphia neighborhood that still bears its name).

colonies, especially in New York, New Jersey, Maryland, and Massachusetts. Some Germans journeyed farther south. For instance, a number of Protestants from the city of Salzburg found a new home in Georgia after Salzburg outlawed Protestantism in 1731.

The colonies also attracted impoverished Germans still reeling from the destruction of the Thirty Years' War. The

Tracing Your Roots

If you are of German ancestry, one of the best and most exciting ways to learn about German-American culture is to study your family. By researching your own German-American roots, you may be able to learn when your ancestors came to America, where they lived in Germany, why they left, and what kind of life they were able to build in their new land. By delving into your family history, you will learn not only about your relatives, but also get a sense of how all immigrants lived and struggled in the United States.

Your first step is to talk with members of your family, especially older relatives. Ask them to share what they know about their parents, grandparents, great-grandparents, and each generation back as far as they have information. Be sure to ask for the birth date and birthplace of each ancestor you can identify. Other important dates you should try to find include dates of death, marriage, divorce, and immigration. Your relatives may have family documents—such as letters, photographs, diaries, bibles, birth certificates, marriage licenses, and wills—from which you can learn a wealth of information. When interviewing relatives, the most important task is to take detailed notes. Be sure not only to write down the facts they provide, but also the source of each piece of information you obtain.

Using your notes, try to compile a pedigree chart, also known as a family tree. This diagram lists the name, birth date, and death date of each relative you have found with lines connecting each generation to the next. Basic genealogical guides in your local public library can help you organize this information. There are also genealogical computer programs available that can help you create a family tree.

To continue your research, visit your local library and ask about what genealogical research resources they have available. Local history and genealogy societies may also be able to guide you in searching through public records for more information. Another excellent source of data is the Internet, which has many websites that allow you to exchange information you have compiled with other researchers.

When studying your German-American ancestors, keep in mind that the borders of German states changed often before Germany was unified in 1871. If you have trouble locating the town or village of an ancestor on the map, try consulting a specialized atlas, such as *Atlas of Central Europe* (John Murray Publishers, 1963).

people of the Palatinate were especially desperate to emigrate. Responding to a rumor that Queen Anne of England would provide free transportation to the colonies, 13,000 Germans from the region fled to London. The English government sent about 2,800 of the Palatinates to New York, where they were put to work making supplies for the English navy.

THE REDEMPTION SYSTEM

Shipping companies took advantage of the eagerness of poor Germans to emigrate by creating the redemption system. If Germans wanted to move to the colonies, but could not afford the fare, the companies allowed them to travel on credit. When the emigrants, known as redemptioners, arrived in North America, they were usually given two weeks to pay back the cost of their passage. If they were unable to do so, they were sold as servants to colonists who agreed to pay their fare in exchange for their labor. Usually, German redemptioners had to work for about four years before they could earn their freedom.

Shipping companies lured redemptioners with extravagant claims. One brochure promised German emigrants that after a just few years in the colonies, "the maid [becomes] a lady, the peasant a nobleman, the artisan a baron." In fact, the redemptioners were left to the mercy of their masters—many of whom treated their charges brutally. The most unscrupulous of them tricked emigrants into signing contracts that made them servants for life. Despite these abuses, the redemption system did not come to an end until 1819, when new American shipping regulations made it unprofitable for shipping companies to transport redemptioners.

GROWTH OF GERMAN POPULATION

As Germans seeking religious and economic freedom fled their native lands, the number of Germans in America grew rapidly. By the 1770s, there were approximately 250,000

Germans in the colonies, making up about 10 percent of the total population. About 30 percent of Pennsylvanians were Germans—a statistic that alarmed one of the colony's leading citizens, Benjamin Franklin. Fearing that Germans might take control over Pennsylvania from the English, he wrote that "unless the stream of importation could be turned from this to other colonies . . . [Germans] will soon outnumber us that all advantages we have will, in my opinion, be not able to preserve our language and even our government will become precarious."

Despite Franklin's concerns, Germans soon proved them-selves loyal friends of the English colonists. Overwhelmingly, Germans supported the English colonists' revolt against their mother country during the American Revolution (1775–1783). Many Germans sympathized with the American colonisits' desire to free themselves from the control of the English government. In Germany, they themselves had resented being ruled by princes, who overtaxed their subjects to finance their extravagant lifestyles. As Francis Daniel Pastorius had complained, "Many thousand Germans, mostly of the nobility . . . are accustomed to follow the vanities of dress, speech, foreign manners and ceremonies, and incur incredible expense in learning to mount, to ride, to dance, to fence . . . while not a single thought is given to the love of God and learning to follow Christ."

GERMANS IN THE AMERICAN REVOLUTION

During the Revolutionary War, thousands of men served in two all-German regiments in Pennsylvania and Maryland. Germans also fought on the side of the English, however. These men were called Hessians. They had been placed in military service by German princes and dukes, who sold their labor to the English. Offering the English a regiment of 600 men, one duke wrote that his soldiers "did not wish for anything better than to find an occasion of sacrificing themselves for the British Majesty." In

In an attempt to stop the American Revolution, England bought the services of many German soldiers (called Hessians) from the German princes and dukes to whom they owed their allegiance. Many Germans in America, however, supported the colonists and fought for American independence in various local and state militias.

fact, the Hessians greatly resented being sent to the colonies to fight on the side of the English. Understandably, they turned out to be less than loyal soldiers. The American army found it could easily persuade the Hessians to join its side. After the Americans won the war, about 12,000 out of 30,000 Hessians chose to stay in the United States and live in German-American settlements.

Aside from the Hessians, few Germans emigrated to the United States during the Revolution. Emigration was again stalled after Napoleon Bonaparte seized control of France in 1799. Setting out to rule all of Europe, Napoleon's armies attacked several German states, bringing about the collapse of the Holy Roman Empire. In 1814, the armies of Prussia and Austria—the two largest German states—helped bring about Napoleon's defeat. At the conclusion of the Napoleonic Wars, the borders of Europe were redrawn. Germany became a confederation of 39 states. But without a strong central government, it remained divided and weak.

POST-WAR BOOM IN GERMAN IMMIGRATION

In the years following the war, the greatest wave of German emigration began. Many Germans had high hopes for their new confederation, but they were soon disappointed. Germany's political power was still in the hands of warring princes, who had little interest in working together to create a united Germany. Germans who wanted to live in a land where average people had a political voice decided to move to America.

Other Germans escaped to America as political refugees in 1848 when revolutions broke out in Austria, France, Italy, and several smaller German states. The revolutionaries wanted to recreate their governments and make them more democratic. The rulers of Europe, however, quickly squelched the revolts. Afraid they would be imprisoned or assassinated, many Germans rebels were forced to flee. A large number of these refugees chose the United States as their destination.

However, most German emigrants in the middle of the nineteenth century left Germany for economic rather than political reasons. By this time, the population of Germany had grown so large that its land could no longer support everyone who lived there. Many families, laboring on small farms of overworked soil, could barely feed themselves.

To survive, some turned to making products such as tools, clocks, and woven cloth. But after the Napoleonic Wars, an international trade developed that brought cheap foreign goods into Germany, leaving most German craftspeople unable to sell their wares. With no means of making a living in their own land, many German families came to see emigrating as their only means of building a decent life.

3　SIX WEEKS TO A BETTER LIFE

DUDEN'S WRITINGS OF AMERICA

In the early 1830s, Gottfried Duden was one of the best-known authors in the German Empire. At the time, many Germans belonged to reading clubs, which met regularly in inns and schoolrooms. During the meetings, one club member read aloud from a book and then the group discussed it. Duden's *Report* was popular with reading clubs throughout Germany because it dealt with a topic that had captured the German imagination—immigration to America.

In the early nineteenth century, more than 150 books about emigration were published in German. But Duden's struck a particular chord with rural Germans. His background gave him an air of authority. Duden was a well-educated lawyer who had held important positions in the government of Prussia. He

Many nineteenth-century German writers like Gottfried Duden extolled the virtues of America's fertile farmland, abundant game, vast mineral deposits, and seemingly limitless space. In the wake of the Napoleonic Wars, many Germans sought to leave their devastated homeland for the promise that America offered.

also was an elegant writer whose enthusiasm for his subject was contagious.

In his *Report*, Duden described his experiences while living in the United States for three years. In 1824, he arrived in Baltimore, Maryland. He then traveled west to Missouri. There, he bought 270 acres of land near where the Mississippi and

Missouri rivers meet and settled into the life of a Missouri farmer. Writes Duden in his *Report*:

> The great fertility of the soil, its immense area, the mild climate, the splendid river connections, the completely unhindered communication in an area of several thousand miles, the perfect safety of person and property, together with very low taxes—all these must be considered as the real foundations for the fortunate situation of Americans.

Duden claimed he found a virtual paradise in Missouri. He wrote glowingly about the natural beauty of his western farm, surrounded by thick forests and clear rivers. Even more enticing to his readers were his descriptions of bountiful harvests and plentiful wild game. According to Duden, once a settler cleared land and built a house, his "whole family lives carefree and happily without a single piece of ready money." Even without farming, a man could easily provide for his wife and children. Duden wrote, "[T]here are so many deer, stag, turkeys, hens, pigeons, pheasants, snipes, and other game that a good hunter without much exertion provides for the needs of a large family."

For many Germans in the 1830s, these were exciting words. Duden's America was a place of beauty and promise, while their own homeland seemed overwhelmed by devastation and hopelessness after the Napoleonic Wars. As it became a daily struggle just to feed themselves, many Germans— especially young adults—became dispirited about their future in their homeland.

Germans who had grown frustrated with Germany's political situation also read Duden's *Report* with interest. German intellectuals and scholars had long dreamed of a united Germany with a representative government. Instead, Germany remained a collection of dozens of small states ruled by princes and dukes, who often imposed large taxes on their subjects. Those eager for a German democracy also wanted to free their people from the traditional German social structure. In Germany, the poor always stayed poor, and the rich always stayed rich. To many impoverished Germans, the ability for Americans to move up in social rank was the most appealing feature of Duden's picture of the United States.

After reading Duden's work, some Germans rushed off to Missouri, only to return with frightening reports of what Duden had left out of his account of life in the American West. Duden said nothing of the constant backbreaking work required to run a farm, possibly because he hired farmhands to perform all the necessary labor on his land. In his description of Missouri, he also neglected to mention the long harsh winters and spring flash floods that constantly threatened the lives and livelihoods of western settlers. German immigrants disillusioned with Duden's overly sunny account of American life called him *Der Lügenhund*, meaning "the lying dog."

The backlash against Duden did little to dampen the Germans' newfound enthusiasm for emigrating. Their interest in leaving their homeland was further encouraged by shipping companies. In the early nineteenth century, innovations in shipping made traveling across the Atlantic faster and safer. By 1830, a ship could cross the ocean in about six weeks. Later in the century, with the introduction of steamships, the voyage took only about 18 days, but few German emigrants had enough money to pay for the higher steamship fares.

In the eighteenth century, most German emigrants had sailed from the French city of Le Havre or the Dutch ports of Rotterdam and Antwerp. But after 1830, the most popular port for German emigration was Bremerhaven in the German state of Bremen. Ships bound for New York City left Bremerhaven on a regular schedule, sailing at the beginning and middle of every month. So many Germans passed through Bremen en route to the United States that it was nicknamed Der Vorort New-Yorks (the suburb of New York).

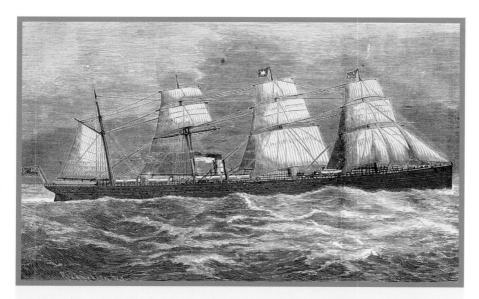

Shipping companies actively recruited German passengers for their freighters returning from Germany to America. Because the cargo on the return trip usually required far less space, passengers were able to travel below decks in primitive accommodations called steerage.

SHIP OWNERS LOOK FOR PASSENGERS

Shipping companies had financial reasons for encouraging German emigration. Sailing from the United States, their ships carried to Europe export goods such as tobacco and cotton, which required a large storage area. On the return trip, they carted European exports, such as tools and linen, which took up much less storage space. Ship owners could therefore increase their profits by filling the excess space in steerage—the cargo area below the deck—with fare-paying emigrants.

To find passengers, the companies sent out agents. These employees signed contracts requiring them to deliver a certain number of emigrants to Bremerhaven on a certain date. The agents traveled from village to village, telling the people there about the advantages of moving to America. They also provided would-be emigrants with information about the trip to Bremerhaven, the voyage across the ocean, and the location of German-American communities already established in the United States. The agents' guidance made emigrating much easier than it had been before.

AMERICA SEEKS GERMAN IMMIGRANTS

By the late nineteenth century, American immigration agents also were working in Germany. Some were employed by railroad companies, especially the Northern Pacific. The U.S. government had granted the Northern Pacific land along its rail routes. The rail company was eager to see this land settled with people who would buy the goods transported by the railroad. German emigrants were particularly targeted by Northern Pacific agents. To convince Germans to settle on their lands, the agents distributed more than 600,000 brochures and advertised in 68 different German newspapers. Northern Pacific also offered German emigrants reduced fares for passage to the United States and operated immigrant houses at town sites near the lands they owned. Newcomers could live at these immigrant houses until their families were able to buy farmland.

Other agents represented American states that wanted to bolster their populations with immigrants. In the late nineteenth century, Wisconsin, Minnesota, Iowa, Nebraska, Kansas, Missouri, Oregon, Montana, and Dakota Territory (now North and South Dakota) all established immigrant boards. Like the railroads, they were especially interested in promoting German immigration. For example, when Wisconsin published a pamphlet to attract immigrants in 1852, it printed 20,000 copies in the German language, but only 5,000 in Norwegian and 4,000 in Dutch. In 1873, Dakota Territory went so far as to name its capital Bismarck after the German chancellor Otto von Bismarck in the hope of luring German immigrants.

States competed for German immigrants for several reasons. In America, Germans were known for being hard-working and law-abiding. Also, many—particularly those who came to the United States to escape religious and political persecution—had more money to spend than most immigrants from other European nations. Sent by the governor of Minnesota to report on conditions for would-be immigrants at Bremerhaven, Albert Wolff wrote in 1870 that "never before [have] I beheld [*sic*] such crowds of emigrants, whose wealth shone forth in their dress and baggage."

LETTERS FROM AMERICA

For the Germans considering emigration, the most important source of information came from letters written by friends and relatives who had already settled in the United States. Immigrants happy in their new homeland soothed fears about the trip to the United States and inspired dreams of building a new and better life there. In one such letter, Josef Riepberger, a recent immigrant living in Cincinnati, Ohio, advised his young relatives in Bavaria to join him in America:

> It is all up to you. I advise all young people to come to America. Their fortunes were ten times better off than in Germany. However, people at the age between 45 and 50 years, who have no children they can rely on, should stay at home in Germany. I thank God a hundred times that I could come to America for I make more money than in Germany and the thought of returning to Germany never comes to mind. My children also do not want to return.

Many letters included more than advice. Once they were established, immigrants often sent family members money so they could also come to America. By the end of the nineteenth century, about one-third of German emigrants had their passages paid by relatives already living in the United States.

My America

In 1875, 16-year-old Wilhelm Bürkert from the German state of Württemburg set off alone for the United States. The following passage from his first letter home describes part of his journey and his first nervous impressions of his new home:

On the 17th of September we arrived in the French city of Havre. In this port there was a 24-hour stop. We were allowed to get off. We looked around this really lovely, large and luxurious city. On Sept. 18th at 10 o'clock in the morning, we departed. But then out on the Atlantic Ocean the ship really started to roll and the waves went clear up to the helmsman. On the same evening, on Saturday the 18th of Sept., I collapsed on the deck. They took me to my berth, where I hit, bit, scratched and ripped all the clothes of the sailors who had to hold me down. They gave me chloroform to put me to sleep. The ship's doctor gave up all hope. On the following Monday they were all waiting for me to die.

Oh, how horrible it is when you don't have anyone. My heart was pounding. They put something on it, it was like fire. The doctor said if he hadn't done that, my heart would have burst. . . .

The last few days we had such a storm that you couldn't stand up or lie down. The trunks we had with us were tied down. The last night we had fog. On the 27th of Sept., or on the Monday, you couldn't see anything at all for 2 nights, the ship went very slowly. The steamwhistles were blown a lot. All at once at 9 o'clock they called out excitedly, Hurray, the pilot. He was coming toward us in a small boat. He had to guide us through the reefs off shore and in through the straits. It was a chief helmsman—almost like a ship's officer. At 4 in the morning we heard land-land. And that is a sight, oh splendid. We were in Stett-Neuland [Staten Island]. Here the anchor was cast. A doctor came out about 7 o'clock and examined each one to see if he had a contagious disease. Everyone was healthy. We were allowed to go on. . . .

Here we all went into a garden where a speech was held. It was Castle-Garden, which is set up to take care of the emigrants. Innkeepers came to offer their services. We went to the inn "Zur Stadt Balingen" [Town of Balingen], the innkeeper is a Württemberger from Balingen. . . .

I got my first job only today, Oct. 2nd, as a waiter and cook. I get food and board and when the month is over, the wages will be decided. Probably 16 dollars = 40 guilders. They won't pay more, that's very little here.

May you all be in good health. You'll write to me soon, won't you? . . . Here in Newjork things are very bad. . . . All the best to you all. New-Jork [*sic*] is 5 times bigger and nicer than Hamburg, and it has 2 million inhabitants, you can get lost easily.

Your thankful son, grandson and brother.

RAISING MONEY FOR PASSAGE

For emigrants without family support, raising the needed money for passage was sometimes difficult. Often, a family had to sell everything they had to pay the fare. Gathering the necessary documents to leave the German Empire was another obstacle. German laws required many emigrants to present baptismal and marriage certificates. Men sometimes also had to prove they had a trade or profession and had served in the army. Emigration officials, however, were not above taking bribes. In one instance, when an official asked an emigrant named Edward Stein for his documents, Stein instead handed the man an envelope full of money. Stein was allowed to leave Germany with no more questions asked.

GETTING TO A PORT

After raising the passage money, an emigrant's first step to reaching the United States was traveling to a port, usually Bremerhaven. The trip could be difficult, especially in the early nineteenth century, before Bremerhaven was accessible by rail. Back then, most emigrants had to make the trip on foot, with their belongings stacked high in rickety carts. In the 1840s, a French journalist wrote about the trail of carts along the main road of Bavaria, where entire villages were setting out for the French port of Le Havre:

> It is a lamentable sight when you are traveling in the spring or autumn on the Strasburg road, to see the long files of carts that you meet every mile, carrying the whole property of the poor wretches . . . their miserable tumbrils [carts]—drawn by such starved, drooping beasts, that your only wonder is, how can they possibly hope to reach Havre alive—piled with the scanty boxes containing their few effects, and on the top of all, the women and children, the sick and bedridden, and all who are too exhausted with the journey to walk.

Equal to the physical demands of the trip was the emotional

pain emigrants felt after saying goodbye to their friends and family, knowing they may never see them again.

Another hazard of the road were con men. Carrying their passage fare, the emigrants were prime targets for swindlers, especially when they were waiting to board their ships at Bremerhaven. According to Albert Wolff, a German emigrant was "preyed upon by blacklegs [cardsharps] and confidence men, here called Bauernfänger, which means trappers of 'green horns,' from the moment he starts from his native city or village."

THE TRIP

The few emigrants able to travel first class could expect a comfortable trip across the ocean. According to an 1843 travel brochure, one wealthy German gentleman occupied a cabin "lined with stained wood, in panels, banded with rose and zebra woods and American bird's-eye maple, and ceiling white and gold." Like other first-class passengers, he was served plenty of fresh meat, milk, and fruit, as well as wine with lunch and dinner.

Most German emigrants, however, could only afford to travel in steerage. Crowded into these dark storage areas, passengers barely had enough room to move without knocking into boxes and barrels of supplies. Appalled by these conditions, charitable organizations pressured the U.S. Congress in 1847 to pass a law specifying that immigrant ships must allow 14 square feet of horizontal space for each passenger. Even when this requirement was met, ships were so overcrowded that many passengers slept in gangways or crude shacks built on the top deck.

In the emigrants' cramped quarters, disease spread quickly, often with deadly results. On one ship sailing from Hamburg, an epidemic of cholera took the lives of 37 out of 286 passengers. Many of the survivors were so ill they had to be carried off the ship after it reached New York.

Nearly all emigrants suffered from lesser ailments, including

Though dank and overcrowded, steerage offered poor German immigrants a chance to reach America cheaply. In 1847, the U.S. Congress set standards for steerage travel that demanded at least 14 feet of horizontal space be provided for each passenger.

scurvy, trench mouth, and body ulcers. Swarms of insects added to their discomfort. Fred Martin, an emigrant who sailed to the United States in 1909, later recalled being awakened by his bawling son: "I examined George's body and found bedbugs crawling about, his body covered with red blotches, and then I knew why he was crying."

Another common complaint of emigrants was the quality of the food and water they were given. After arriving in New York, one German immigrant bitterly recalled the lack of decent food aboard his ship: "After two weeks, the potatoes gave out; the peas were musty, the meat and butter spoiled and had to be thrown into the sea. The passengers lived on hard branny bread, prunes and watery barley soup." Unlike immigrant ships from other countries, most German vessels had a cooking staff to provide meals for the passengers, so they did not have to cook in their crowded steerage quarters. Passengers, however, were expected to help the ship's crew by assisting the cooks, washing linens, or mopping the deck. German ship captains also insisted that passengers come to the deck for daily exercise sessions.

Passengers were excused from exercise only when ships ran into stormy weather. When storms rocked these vessels, many people became seasick, filling the ship with the stench of vomit. In steerage, rough waters sent people and their possessions flying. In a letter to her relatives back home, emigrant Angela Heck wrote of a particularly harrowing storm at sea in 1854:

> The ship was listing to one side and all the top planks started to break. We had to hold on as tight as we could to keep from falling out. . . . The ship started to crack, two masts broke and their sails and ropes were ripped and torn to pieces. Then the ship sank down very deep and water came into the opening like it was being poured in with a bucket. . . . We were all so frightened we couldn't even pray. We repented our sins and we all prepared to die.

ARRIVAL IN NEW YORK CITY AND OTHER PORTS

Understandably, emigrants were relieved when they finally reached the United States. Although large numbers of Germans sailed to Baltimore, New Orleans, and other port cities, the most popular destination was New York City.

When a ship arrived in New York, health officials checked each passenger to ensure that no infectious diseases were brought into the country. Immigrants often had to endure a day's quarantine before being allowed to set foot on American soil.

When a ship arrived in New York, no one was allowed to disembark until health inspectors examined the passengers and determined they were not carrying any infectious diseases. Theodor Engelmann, a German who arrived in New York in 1833, later wrote of how he nervously awaited permission to leave the ship:

> [T]he sun rose in a cloudless sky and illuminated with her magic light the bay with its charming shores and the city in the distance. . . . We had to spend one day in painful quarantine in sight of the long expected landing before we were allowed to set foot on firm land and to go into the city of New York.

After 1855, Germans arriving in New York were sent to the immigration station at Castle Garden, located off the southern tip of Manhattan. (A new immigration station on Ellis Island opened in 1892, but by then the largest wave of German immigration was over. Still, about 1.5 million German immigrants passed through Ellis Island before it closed in 1954.) At Castle Garden, immigrants were provided with information about where to stay in the city while they looked for work or made plans to join relatives in another area of the country.

Many immigrants were given aid by the German Society of New York City. Founded in 1784 and funded by prosperous German Americans, the society was a charitable organization that offered advice, emergency financial support, and information about jobs. For many Germans, overwhelmed by the bustling city filled with English-speakers, the society provided something even more essential—the comfort of seeing a friendly face and hearing a familiar language before heading off on their adventure in America.

4

THE OLD COUNTRY IN THE NEW WORLD

Johann C. W. Pritzlaff was one of the Germans who came to the United States during the greatest wave of German immigration, which occurred between 1830 and 1890. In 1842, Pritzlaff wrote in a letter to his German relatives:

America is a good country, it blossoms under God's blessing, but it bears thorns and thistles as well. For a man who works, it is much better that [sic] in Germany, one doesn't live so restrictedly and in such servitude as you do under the great estate-owners. . . . There is quite a fair amount of equality among men here in America. The high and wealthy are not ashamed to associate with the poor and lowly. . . . As far [sic] church matters go, I cannot write much that is good, for the Antichrist has also set up his See [sic] in America. But the best thing here is that everyone has the freedom to act according to his own belief. He who follows false teachings does so of his own free will.

During this period, nearly 4.5 million Germans arrived in America. After surviving the difficult ocean journey, these immigrants faced the challenge of making their way in a new land. Like Pritzlaff, they proved astute critics of the United States, embracing the "blossoms" while rejecting the "thorns and thistles" they discovered in the American way of life.

As in earlier centuries, many German immigrants who arrived in the middle of the nineteenth century were farmers, attracted to America by the lure of cheap or even free land. In fact, about 27 percent of all German immigrants were farmers in 1870. The percentage of farmers, however, was smaller than that of most other immigrant groups. Among the Germans were an unusually large number of skilled workers and trades-people. Many German immigrants were weavers, cabinetmakers, carpenters, cobblers, and bookbinders. Others were merchants,

Many of those who arrived in America during the largest wave of German immigration (1830-1890) were farmers. Lured by the promise of cheap land, they quickly planted crops in fields like this one, using horse-drawn carts and steam-powered threshing engines to bring in their harvest.

Soon after their arrival in America, German immigrants quickly dominated the brewing profession. German-owned breweries like this one quickly sprang up, including those bearing the now familiar names of Pabst, Schlitz, and Busch.

bakers, tailors, and gardeners. Germans soon dominated certain professions in the United States, especially printing and brewing. German breweries—such as Pabst and Schlitz in Milwaukee, Wisconsin, and Busch in St. Louis, Missouri— eventually made enormous fortunes for their owners. As time passed, the makeup of German immigrants gradually changed. Throughout the nineteenth century, more and more Germans immigrants were unskilled laborers. By 1890, they made up 45 percent of all Germans entering America.

GEOGRAPHIC DISTRIBUTION OF GERMAN SETTLEMENT

In the colonial period, most German immigrants settled in a large region in the northeastern United States. The area roughly formed a triangle stretching from Ohio in the west to New York in the north to Virginia in the south. As the great wave of German immigration began in the 1830s, however, Germans started heading farther west, moving into the Ohio River Valley and the Great Lakes region. Farmers settled in rural areas, whereas many tradespeople flocked to Chicago, Detroit, Milwaukee, Cincinnati, and other urban centers that grew up in these regions. Germans also continued to settle in cities along the Atlantic Coast, including New York, Baltimore, and Philadelphia.

Generally, Germans stayed in the Northeast and Midwest. A few German-American communities emerged in other areas, however. For instance, Germans began settling in rural Texas in the 1820s, when the area was still part of Mexico. Texas was then largely unsettled by non-Indians. The Mexican government feared that the United States might try to take over the region unless Mexico was able to entice settlers to make their homes there. Unable to convince many Mexicans to move north into Texas, Mexico looked to settlers from other lands, including Germany.

In 1831, the Mexican government gave Friedrich Ernst from the city of Oldenburg a sizable land grant in what is now Austin County, Texas. Ernst wrote a friend, telling him how beautiful and fertile his lands were. The letter was published in an Oldenburg newspaper, planted there by a business founded to establish German settlements in Texas. For a flat fee, it transported emigrants across the ocean and gave them land, a house, and the tools they needed to start a farm. The offer attracted 7,000 customers before the firm went bankrupt after two years in operation. Nevertheless, Texas settlements continued to attract German immigrants. A total of about 30,000 Germans arrived in Texas before the 1860s. Many settled in the German towns of New Braunfels and Fredericksburg.

California also attracted German immigrants in the 1830s and 1840s. Among them was John A. Sutter, a businessman who was born in the German state of Baden. Near the present-day city of Sacramento, he founded the settlement of New

Helvetia, where some 300 settlers made a living through cattle ranching and wheat farming. In 1848, an employee of Sutter's discovered gold on his land. News of the gold spread quickly, sparking the California Gold Rush. People from around the world rushed to the area, hoping to make their fortune. Some Germans joined the rush, but most were merchants. One such German emigrant, Levi Strauss, became rich, but not because he struck gold. Instead, Strauss built a successful business selling durable pants made from canvas and denim to goldseekers. These durable pants, which later became known as blue jeans, gained such popularity that Strauss' company still thrives today.

LATIN FARMERS

Another area of German settlement was Missouri. In the 1830s, the writings of Gottfried Duden described the area in such glowing terms that they helped spark the major wave of German immigration. Thousands of those immigrants decided they wanted not only to move to the United States, but to live in the exact area Duden had described. Among the Missouri emigrants were many wealthy gentlemen, including a number of counts and barons. They had romantic notions about the spiritual satisfactions of working the land, but were wholly unprepared for the reality of farming. Ill-suited to hard physical labor, they were mocked by other settlers. They called these German gentlemen "Latin farmers," a reference to their classical education in the Latin language.

Many Latin farmers and other German intellectuals saw immigration as more than just a means for their countrymen to better their economic lot. These Germans had given up hope that Germany could become a democratic country, so they envisioned an American Germania—an all-German state established within the United States—as the next best thing. Giessener Gesellschaft was one society formed to foster the development of such a German state in Missouri. As its leaders declared, "the foundation of a new and free Germany in the

In the late eighteenth century, the Russian army began attempting to recruit pacifist German Mennonites for military service, violating a promise made to the Mennonites by Catherine the Great (the Prussian-born empress of Russia). As a result, many fled to the United States, settling predominantly in the Midwest.

great North American Republic shall be laid by us." Their dream was never realized, but they did succeed in encouraging still more immigration to Missouri.

RUSSIAN GERMANS

Far more skilled than Missouri's Latin farmers were the large number of Russian Germans who began immigrating to the Midwest in the 1870s. These immigrants were the ancestors of Germans who had moved to Russia in the middle of the eighteenth century at the invitation of Catherine the Great, the Russian Empress who was herself a German. Catherine offered Germans land and religious freedom if they settled in the southern part of the Russian Empire, which she wanted to populate with devoted citizens. Most of the Germans who resettled in Russia were Mennonites. Their religion condemned committing any violent act, so Catherine promised they would not have to serve in the Russian army. A century later, however, the Russian government reneged on the agreement and began rounding up German men for military service. In 1909, a Russian German named Pauline Neher Diede told the story of what had happened to her father Ludwig:

> Cossacks [Russian cavalrymen] had been riding through village streets picking up young men without serving them notice. Mothers cried and screamed at them. Ludwig hardly had time to say good-by to his mother and gather up a few belongings. . . . He served about a year, through a record cold winter and an especially sweltering summer. He saw two buddies killed, and another severely wounded.

To escape the draft, thousands of Russian Germans headed to the United States. Most settled in western states, such as Nebraska, Kansas, and the Dakotas. These immigrants brought with them seeds of a winter wheat native to Turkey. Able to survive the harsh winters, this strain of wheat grew well in the Great Plains. The contributions of Russian Germans helped make the Plains states leading wheat producers, earning the area the nickname "America's Breadbasket."

For all Germans settling in the rural west, starting a farm was a challenge. After acquiring land, an immigrant family had to begin the hard work of building a house and clearing fields of trees and rocks so that it could be plowed. Men, women, and children all labored together, working long hours to ensure an adequate harvest. For some, the harshness of farm life came as a shock. Rosa Kleberg, a German farm wife who arrived in

Texas in 1834, wrote of her family's difficult adjustment to their new surroundings:

> Circumstances were very different from what we expected. My brothers had pictured pioneer life as one of hunting and fishing, and it was hard for them to settle down to the drudgery and toil of splitting rails and cultivating the field, work which was entirely new to them.

The unrelenting labor required for farming destroyed the health of many German immigrants. Sophia Kallenberger Beck, a Russian German who emigrated to South Dakota in 1877, later wrote of her mother's enormous physical suffering while establishing their family farm:

> Not only did she look after her household and the hundreds of duties there, she was expected to be the first hand help with outdoor work. Her day began at dawn and did not end until the small hours. The family's livelihood often demanded of a woman something beyond human endurance. Cooking and sewing for large families turned women into old ladies before their time.

FINDING WORK IN CITIES

German immigrants in cities also faced many obstacles to establishing themselves in their new country. Finding work was often difficult, even for skilled tradesmen. In 1855, a German weaver named Martin Weitz wrote his father of his suicidal desperation before finding a job in Hartford, Connecticut: "I am now very content with my situation, I'll stay here. Last winter sometimes I just wanted to jump into the water, if you don't have a job in America it's a terrible thing, I can't thank God enough that I have work and am healthy."

After locating work, German immigrants often found themselves at the mercy of unscrupulous employers. An 1884 article in the *Chicagoer Arbeiter-Zeitung,* a German-language newspaper, included a young woman's account of how a factory owner had taken advantage of her and her coworkers:

> When we started several weeks ago, Mr. Bonde promised us $2.50 a week. But shortly afterwards he came and said that we had to do piecework. Then he set the prices so that even if we worked as hard as we could, we could barely earn $1.50. We complained and got a raise. . . . But we didn't receive the money we had earned.

ADJUSTING TO AMERICAN CUSTOMS

German immigrants also struggled to adjust to American customs and ideas. Americans struck many Germans as crude and brash, more interested in making money than anything else. As Martin Weitz observed, even churchgoing Americans had few qualms about cheating others in business:

> There is just as much roguery over here, it knows no bounds, the Americans go to Schochs [church] . . . 3 times every Sunday and 3 evenings a week, and they think they're so holy but when they can take the skin off the back of someone else they don't mind at all. These people just pray to get what they want, that's what the Americans are like.

Many Germans were also baffled by the relationships among family members in America. In Germany, the father was the undisputed ruler of the household. His wife and children were expected to bow to his wishes. In the Germans' eyes, American men allowed women and children far too much freedom. In a letter to relatives in the old country, one immigrant complained about the status of women in the United States:

> The general respect for womanhood causes parents to spoil their daughters and neglect teaching them the necessary skills for managing a household. It is little wonder that they often attend such ridiculous women's rights conventions where they

praise women's noble position in society, even though one can find nowhere else so few good housewives as in America. . . . The husbands let the wives become rulers of the house.

Seeing the way American women were regarded, some German wives rebelled against their husbands. For instance, a farmer named Christian Lenz wrote his brother about the breakup of a friend's marriage, attributing the split to the husband's abuse of his wife:

> I've heard it was his fault, he beat his wife for every little thing, and that's not done here, here a wife must be treated like a wife and not like a scrub rag like I saw in Germany so often that a man can do what he wants to with his wife. He who likes to beat his wife had better stay in Germany, it doesn't work here.

However, most German women were content with their traditional roles, even after emigrating. Their lives continued to revolve around "Kirche, Kinder, Küche"—church, children, and the kitchen. Many German women did not work outside of the home. Those who did were usually employed in family-run businesses. German children often left school early so they could also work with their families.

LITTLE GERMANIES

In general, Germans were slower to adopt American customs than many other immigrant groups, largely because they did not need to. In both the city and the country, German immigrants tended to live in all-German settlements, where they could re-create the way of life they knew in the old country. In cities such as New York, Chicago, Cincinnati, Milwaukee, St. Louis, and Baltimore, many *Kleindeutschlands* (Little Germanies) grew up. Walking through these neighborhoods, immigrants could see many familiar sites. There were stores filled with German books and newspapers. There were theaters with German acting troupes performing the works of Johann

Wolfgang von Goethe, Friedrich von Schiller, and other famous German playwrights. There were beer halls, where families gathered to socialize and sing old folk songs. There were also outside markets, where the air was filled with both the comforting smells of wurst (sausage), sauerkraut, and other traditional foods and the reassuring sound of the German language. Living in a Little Germany, an immigrant could almost feel as though he had never left home. As a Danish writer in Milwaukee noted in the 1850s, "many Germans live here who never learn English, and seldom go beyond the German town."

SOCIAL CLUBS

Wherever they settled in America, Germans established *Vereine,* or social clubs. Early clubs had practical functions. Most were

How Others Saw Them

J. Hector St. John de Crèvecoeur in his *Letters from an American Farmer* (1782) on the resilience of eighteenth-century German immigrants: "How much wiser, in general, the honest Germans than almost all other Europeans; they hire themselves to some of their wealthy landsmen, and in that apprenticeship learn everything that is necessary. . . . Their astonishment at their first arrival from Germany is very great—it is to them a dream; the contrast must be powerful indeed; they observe their countrymen flourishing in every place; they travel through whole counties where not a word of English is spoken; and in the names and the language of the people, they retrace Germany. . . . The recollection of their former poverty and slavery never quits them as long as they live."

President Theodore Roosevelt in a 1903 speech, praising German Americans for the role they played in the Civil War: "In the Civil War it would be difficult to paint in too strong colors what I may well-nigh call the all-importance of the American citizens of German birth and extraction toward the cause of the Union and liberty, especially in what were then known as border states. It would have been out of the question to have kept Missouri loyal had it not been for the German element therein."

Among the most prominent of German-American social organizations were the *Turnvereine* (Turner Societies). Begun as physical fitness clubs, these societies encouraged the values of hard work and cleanliness. Later, they began to exert a considerable influence over local politics and the German-language press.

mutual aid societies that provided financial assistance and medical care for members in need. As German immigration increased, clubs were founded purely to organize social and cultural events. Some were open only to people from certain areas of Germany, but most were built around specific activities.

Among the most popular clubs were *Gesangvereine*, or singing societies. Members of these groups gathered to sing folk songs and to play classical music. Several times a year, all of the Gesangvereine in an area came together for a *Sängerfest* (singing festival), where singers and musicians would compete with one another.

Another type of club established by German Americans were *Turnvereine*, or Turner Societies. These organizations grew out of teachings of Friedrich Ludwig Jahn, a political figure who advocated the establishment of a unified Germany in the early nineteenth century. Jahn also stressed to his followers the importance of physical fitness through gymnastics.

The *Turnvereine* founded in the United States were essentially gymnastics clubs, but they also had a political component. Many club members had been involved in the revolutions of 1848 and continued to espouse progressive political beliefs after arriving in the United States. Although these so-called Forty-Eighters numbered only a few thousand, they had a great influence on German-American communities, in large part through their participation in the German-language press. By the late nineteenth century, newspapers printed in German were established in every American city where German immigrants settled. At their height in the 1890s, the German press in the United States published more than 800 papers.

PRESERVING THE GERMAN LANGUAGE

Many German-language newspapers were published by religious organizations. Believing that "language saves the faith," German-American clergy felt that the use of German was crucial to retaining old religious traditions in their new homeland. In their eyes, the English language was a corrupting force. For instance, Reverend Anton H. Walburg, a German-American clergyman in Cincinnati, wrote in 1889 that "a foreigner who loses his nationality is in danger of losing his faith and character. When the German immigrant . . . seeks to throw aside his nationality . . . the first word he learns is generally a curse." To preserve their native language, German-American ministers and priests delivered their services in German. They also did so out of fear that if they began using English, there would be nothing to keep their congregations from joining other more established American churches.

German Catholics were particularly insistent on the use of German in church. In the United States, most Catholic immigrants were Irish. Not wanting to be dominated by the Irish, who shared their faith, German Catholics struggled to maintain their independence by operating their own churches with services in their native tongue.

Schools also played an important role in preserving German. Many German-American communities operated their own schools. In Ohio, Wisconsin, Indiana, and other states where there was a large German-American population, Germans succeeded in persuading public school systems to offer classes in the German language.

Many German-American families were also intent on preserving their language traditions. Parents and children alike learned to speak English so they could communicate with business associates and classmates. Yet, in their homes, many continued to use the language of their ancestors. In his autobiography, writer Hermann Hagedorn told this anecdote about his German immigrant father:

> The girls and I generally talked English with Mother, but, when Father was around, and especially at the dinner-table, the language was German. Occasionally, if we were forgetful or obdurate, slipping into English, or returning to German too tardily, the paternal fist would make the dishes rattle with an emphatic but good-natured "*Hier wird deutsch gesprochen!*" [Here, German is spoken!]

Even when Hagedorn grew impatient with his father's rules, he realized his father only wanted his children to retain a sense of their German heritage. "Talking German seemed to us somehow strained," Hagedorn wrote, adding, "but Father was right, of course, when he said someday we would be glad he had been strict about it."

5

A DIVIDED PEOPLE

"To America," cries the madcap gaily and audaciously, defiant against the first sad hour which will put his strength to the test . . . — "to America," whispers the desperate man who here on the margin of ruin was being pulled, slowly but surely, toward the abyss — "to America," says the poor man, softly and resolutely, who again and again had struggled with manly strength, put futilely against the power of circumstances . . . — "to America," laughs the criminal after his successfully perpetrated robbery . . . — "to America," exults the idealist, spurning the real world . . . hoping for a world over there across the ocean which matches the one produced in his own frantic brain.

—**Friedrich Gerstaecker,** *Nach Amerika!*

Although they shared a common homeland, the Germans who chose to migrate to the United States were widely varied in their religion, social status, and background. Noblemen, peasants, scholars, and tradesmen all sought to enrich their lives in America.

In his popular book, *Nach Amerika!* (*To America!*), author Friedrich Gerstaecker marveled at the wide spectrum of Germans who chose to emigrate to the United States. Numbering in the millions, German Americans were a varied group, representing an enormous range of backgrounds, interests, goals, and philosophies. Some German Americans were rich noblemen, and others were poor peasants. Some were learned scholars, and others were completely uneducated. Some were Catholics, some were Jews, and some were Protestants. Hardly a homogeneous people, German Americans often were as different from one another in their beliefs and customs as they were from non-German Americans.

CLUB GERMANS AND CHURCH GERMANS

One of the most significant divisions in German-American society was that between the "Club Germans" and the "Church Germans." The lives of Club Germans revolved around their participation in social and cultural organizations, whereas those of the Church Germans were centered on church activities. Club Germans primarily lived in urban areas, while Church Germans generally worked on farms. Often struggling farmers and craftspeople, Church Germans tended to be more conservative and isolated from American society. Club Germans in cities—even those living in Little Germanies—had daily contact with people from other ethnic groups. Church Germans in rural areas, however, generally stayed within their communities, only occasionally encountering German Americans from other settlements and rarely meeting any non-Germans at all.

THE GRAYS AND THE GREENS

German Americans were also divided between the Grays and the Greens. The Grays were the settlers who arrived in the United States in the early nineteenth century. Most came to America to escape religious oppression or to better their economic situation. The Greens, also known as the Forty-Eighters, were the immigrants who left Germany after the failed revolutions of 1848. Some fled to the United States to escape arrest and imprisonment, while others were lured to America by the promise of political freedoms they could not expect to have in their native land.

GERMANS AND AMERICAN POLITICS

Before the arrival of the Forty-Eighters, most German Americans shied away from politics. Because of their large population, German Americans probably could have been elected to positions of power, especially in states where they were highly concentrated. But there were several obstacles to

German-American political involvement. Many immigrants were poor when they arrived in the United States. Understandably, they were more inclined to invest their time and effort in building farms and businesses than in seeing German-American officials elected. Many German Americans also did not fully understand the voting and election process in the United States. They came from non-democratic states ruled by princes, not by elected representatives. Language was another hurdle to participation in politics. Many German-born immigrants had little or no knowledge of English, effectively barring them from becoming active members in the American political system.

Nevertheless, the Grays were occasionally drawn into politics by reform efforts that threatened their freedom to live as they wished. Some American reformers, for instance, campaigned for temperance—that is, restricting the consumption of alcohol. Germans opposed temperance, since much of their social lives revolved around beer halls and beer taverns. They also fought laws against breaking the Sabbath. Many Americans believed that Sunday should be reserved for religious activities only. Most Germans, however, favored what Americans called "Continental Sundays." As was common on the continent of Europe, Germans spent Sunday afternoons with their families, often drinking, feasting, hiking, and listening to music outdoors. Elsie Mohr, a German American who grew up in Nebraska and Minnesota in the late nineteenth century, described the pleasures of her family's Sunday get-togethers to an interviewer in 1974:

> [T]hey'd go together on Sunday afternoons, they'd have a party and they'd have a keg of beer and those men would sit around under the trees in the summer time, and they had their beer and they'd sing songs or they'd play cards. And the women too, they really enjoyed it. Everybody was so neighborly you know.

What German Americans saw as a pleasurable way of spending time with friends and relatives, however, was regarded as blasphemous by some American Christians.

The local beer hall or village feast provided a center for social activity in many German-American communities. While many Americans argued for temperance (eventually resulting in Prohibition), German Americans steadfastly opposed the movement.

HOSTILITY OF NATIVISTS

The efforts to regulate German social customs were part of the larger Nativist movement that grew up in the United States in the 1840s and 1850s. Nativists blamed all America's problems on the large number of immigrants coming to its shores. They wanted to restrict immigration and believed that mainstream American customs were superior to all foreign ways. Nativists were also stridently anti-Catholic. They eventually formed their own political party. Officially known as the

American Party, it was nicknamed the Know-Nothing Party, because the secretive organization told members to say they knew nothing when asked about the party's plans and beliefs.

Nativist opposition to immigrants sometimes prompted bloodshed. To protect themselves, some German-American communities formed their own militias. One of the worst incidences of violence against Germans occurred in Louisville, Kentucky, in August 1855. Farmer Christian Lenz wrote his relatives in Germany about how Germans and Irish were beaten when they tried to cast votes in a local election:

> I already wrote you in the last letter that the Germans are unwanted in America, but from last February till now it's cost a lot of blood, on August 6th there was an election in Louisville where they had it in for the Germans and those from Aireland [Ireland], they wanted to cast their votes like always but they got beaten and pushed around, then there was a real fight with much bloodshed. . . . Now dear brother should anyone else move to America, no—stay where you were born that is your home, if I were still in Germany I wouldn't look at America, even if there's nothing besides bread and potatoes and salt that is still better than meat three times a day in a foreign country.

As the fighting against German and Irish immigrants raged through the streets of Louisville, 22 people were killed and hundreds were injured.

German-American political involvement grew in the 1850s, not only as a reaction against Nativism, but also because of the arrival of the Forty-Eighters. Many of them were scholars and intellectuals who had been politically active in Germany. Naturally, once they came to the United States, they were eager to take their place in American political life. Although they numbered only a few thousand, the Forty-Eighters became a powerful voice both in the German-American community and in American society at large.

The Haymarket Riot

On May 3, 1886, Chicago police broke up a strike by laborers petitioning for an eight-hour workday at McCormick Harvesting Machine Company. Under the captain's orders, the policemen fired into the crowd, killing one striker and injuring several others. The appalled strike leaders organized a protest. The following day, about 2,500 people gathered in Haymarket Square. Several of the protest speakers were German Americans, including August Spies, influential editor of the German-language publication *Die Arbeiter-Zeitung* (*The Worker's Newspaper*). The crowd listened to the speeches and left around 10 P.M.

Despite a peaceful protest, Chicago police arrived while 200 attendees were still milling around. A bomb suddenly exploded and the panicked police fired into the crowd. Seven policemen were killed, most by their fellow officers' bullets. At least four workers died; about 60 others were injured.

Responding to the stunned public's demand that the bomb thrower be found and punished, the police arrested labor movement leaders. Ten men were indicted, including eight German Americans. Eight of the men, including Spies, were brought to trial. The prosecution had no proof that they were involved in the bombing. In fact, several were not even at the rally. But the facts of the case mattered little to the staunchly anti-labor judge, Joseph E. Gary, who refused the defense counsel's right to present crucial evidence. Eight defendants were found guilty of murder. Gary sentenced one defendant to 15 years in prison and the rest to death by hanging.

After several unsuccessful appeals, one of the convicted men committed suicide before the executions scheduled for November 11, 1887. The governor of Illinois lessened the sentences of three other men to life in prison. Spies and the remaining three were executed on what labor leaders came to call Black Friday. Their bodies were buried together in German Waldheim Cemetery in Forest Park, Illinois.

On June 24, 1893, Illinois' new governor, the German immigrant John Peter Altgeld, pardoned the three surviving defendants. Altgeld documented the injustices of the Haymarket trial, stating, "the judge was biased, the jury packed, the defendants not proved guilty."

A day after Altgeld's pardon, a crowd of 8,000 gathered at German Waldheim Cemetery for speeches about the three executed men who lost their lives for the labor movement. The speeches led to the dedication of the Haymarket Martyr's Monument. The base bears the last words August Spies spoke: "The day will come when our silence will be more powerful than the voices you are throttling today."

Some Forty-Eighters wanted to form their own all-German political party. In 1858, one Green newspaper editor argued that this would be the best way to combat Nativism:

> If the nativists have a right to found a party which is all Anglo-Saxon, we must have a right to have ours all German. . . . The German element should take the initiative, become the leverage of reform in American politics. The German would hold the balance of power in American politics and become the guardian of both German national and American national interests.

The Forty-Eighters instead ended up throwing their support to the new Republican Party. Most Grays were Democrats, believing that the Democratic Party was most sympathetic to the common man. The Forty-Eighters, however, were drawn to the Republicans because of their anti-slavery beliefs. Having suffered under the hands of dictatorial German princes, many German Americans were against slavery, but the politically progressive Forty-Eighters were particularly passionate about the issue.

GERMANS AND THE REPUBLICAN PARTY

During the 1860 presidential election campaign, the Republicans recognized that German Americans could help their cause. They actively courted German immigrant voters by adopting a platform nicknamed the "Dutch plank." (Germans had long been erroneously called Dutch—a mispronunciation of *Deutsch,* which means *German* in the German language.) The Dutch plank was anti-Nativist. It specifically condemned a controversial law passed in Massachusetts that made it more difficult for immigrants to become U.S. citizens. The plank also supported offering free land to settlers in western states—a measure attractive to Germans eager to start their own farms. The offer would become law after the election with the passage of the Homestead Act of 1862.

Many Germans were won over to the Republican Party. One convert was immigrant Martin Weitz, who, in a letter to his German relatives, explained how German Americans were caught up in the slavery debate:

> As far as America is concerned, things have come to a bad point, here it's all about slavery or freedom. There were 2 parties here, the Democratic and the Republican, things always used to be ruled by the Democrats here, but it is no good any longer, so another party has risen up, namely the Republican party. It is against slavery and that's a good thing which I worked for too, there were great public meetings held on both sides. . . . But many of our German countrymen who were democratically minded over there, they say I was a Democrat in Germany, my father was a Democrat and so I will remain one too. But they don't think very far for they voted with the slaveholders.

Some historians believe that German Americans essentially decided the 1860 election. These scholars hold that without the support of German Americans, the Republican candidate—Abraham Lincoln—would not have been elected president.

GERMAN AMERICANS IN THE CIVIL WAR

Soon after Lincoln's election, the national controversy over slavery came to a head. Eleven slave-holding states in the southern United States declared their independence and formed a new nation they called the Confederacy. Their action prompted the American Civil War (1861–1865). Most German Americans sided with the Union, as the northern states were called. The widespread opposition to slavery among German immigrants was one factor in their support. But just as important was the geography of German immigration. Since most German Americans lived in the Northeast and Midwest, they naturally felt an allegiance to the Union.

Many historians believe that German Americans were critical to Abraham Lincoln's victory in the election of 1860. A fundamental opposition to slavery won many German immigrants over to the Republican cause.

German-American men signed up in large numbers to fight for the North. More than 175,000 German Americans eventually joined the Union army. Many were in the nearly 30 all-German regiments. Often, groups of men enlisted *en masse* (in a large group). For example, an entire militia unit or singing society sometimes chose to go to war. Members of Turner Societies were particularly eager recruits. More than 50 percent of the Turners fought in the war.

During the fighting, German Americans distinguished themselves as skillful soldiers in battle. Confederate general Robert E. Lee even said, "Take the Dutch [the Germans] out of the Union army and we could whip the Yankees [the Northerners] easily." After the war ended with a Union victory, all German Americans benefited from the gratitude other loyal Americans felt for their contribution to the war effort. After years of fighting Nativist reformers, German Americans had regained their reputation as a respected and valued immigrant population.

For many individual German-American soldiers, the war was a boon. This was especially true for young recent immigrants. Often without jobs or family nearby to give them financial aid, they signed up for the army to collect a military salary—money they desperately needed to survive until they became more settled. Some of these men had already served in German armies and therefore felt comfortable with the soldier's life. One enthusiastic German-American soldier named Ferdinand Cunz wrote his father about the attack on the *Merrimack,* a Confederate warship, in 1862:

> Across Norfolk Bay comes a ship flying the rebel flag. . . . All bullets from our batteries fell like peas from the side of the ironclad Merrimack and in half an hour our beautiful frigate Cumberland with 200 men aboard was sunk. . . . From all directions now came enemy gun boats and opened fire on our camp. . . . Until 6 o'clock at night the firing continued but the rain of bombshells went over our camp. This was surely the greatest spectacle ever before witnessed in the world. I would not have missed it for five hundred dollars. . . .

But other German-American soldiers were shattered by

Outside of the Castle Garden immigration station, the Union signs up potential soldiers, including newly arrived German immigrants. During the Civil War, German Americans distinguished themselves as loyal and fierce soldiers for the Union army.

their war experiences. In 1865, farmer Christian Lenz wrote home about the horrors of battle:

> I was a soldier for 9 months, saw many things, was in 3 battles.
> . . . Dear brother those were hard days for us, the last two days
> we had to take their stronghold by storm, the enemy had over
> 100 cannons aimed at us and thousands of guns and we still had
> to take it, they fell to the left and to the right of me, but the Lord
> brought me through safely and brought me back to my family.

WAR AND UNIFICATION OF GERMANY

Soon after the end of the Civil War, German Americans turned their attention to another conflict—one being fought in the fatherland. During the early 1860s, Otto von Bismarck had become the prime minister of Prussia. He slowly worked to build up the Prussian army, helping to make Prussia the most

For centuries, Germany had been a collection of small city-states, each ruled by a local prince or nobleman. Following his successful campaign against the French in the 1860s, Otto von Bismarck (then prime minister of Prussia) was able to pressure the leaders of the smaller states to form a unified Germany.

powerful of all the German states. In 1870, the Prussians entered a war with the French. As the Prussian army invaded France, German Americans anxiously awaited news from the battlefront. Each German victory filled them not only with relief but also with pride, as farmer Christian Lenz explained in a letter to his brother in the old country:

> Here in Amirüka [America] all you hear is what comes from Germany, namely the war, the Germans are all enthusiastic about Germany, thousands of talers [German coins] were collected and sent to Germany for widows and orphans and cripples or the wounded. . . . Many a prayer is sent from the pulpits here by the preachers and other people up to God, that God may give victory to Germany for we believe that Germany is in the right. . . . [I]f Germany wins that will also be a victory for all Germans wherever they are in the whole world.

Within months, Bismarck emerged victorious. Impressed by the display of Prussia's power, he was able to pressure the rulers of other German states to form a unified Germany with Bismarck as its chancellor and William I of Prussia as its emperor. Long the dream of many German Americans, the unification of Germany was celebrated throughout the United States. Great parades were held in New York, Chicago, Cleveland, St. Louis, and other major cities. They featured displays and floats touting the many contributions Germans had made to American life. German veterans also marched down parade routes to remind other Americans of the sacrifices they had made during the Civil War.

In celebrating the unification of Germany, German Americans became unified. At least for a moment, the divisions in German-American society were forgotten. There were no longer Grays and Greens, or Club Germans and Church Germans. There were only German Americans—a great and proud people united both by their embrace of the United States and by their continued love of their German homeland.

6

THE WORLD WARS

We German-Americans are the hyphen between Germany and America; we present the living demonstration of the fact that a large population may be transplanted from one to another country and may be devoted to the new fatherland for life and death.

**—German-American politician Carl Schurz,
in a speech given at the Louisiana Purchase Exposition of 1904**

On October 6, 1883, German Americans observed the 200th anniversary of the founding of Germantown, Pennsylvania, the first German settlement in the United States. The event encouraged German-American groups to make the date an annual holiday. By the 1890s, German Day was celebrated in cities across the country.

Among the best-known German Americans of the late ninteenth and early twentieth centuries was Carl Schurz, who served as both a U.S. senator and as secretary of the interior.

CELEBRATION OF GERMAN DAY

A particularly spectacular German Day celebration was held in 1904 in St. Louis, Missouri, the site of the Louisiana Purchase Exposition. This great fair attracted visitors from all over the world. The main speaker at the German Day festivities was Carl Schurz, one of the best-known German Americans of his time. During his political career, Schurz served as a U.S. senator and as the secretary of the interior, in addition to being a close adviser to President Abraham Lincoln. To a large crowd, Schurz spoke of the pride of German Americans in both their past and

Carl Schurz

A journalist, soldier, and statesman, Carl Schurz was one of the most influential men in nineteenth-century American politics. Born in Liblar, Germany, in 1829, Schurz dreamed of becoming a history professor. Toward that goal, he entered the University of Bonn in 1847. But soon his studies were put aside as he was swept up in a student-led revolution to overthrow the rule of German princes and establish a democratic government in Germany. The revolutionary army, however, was quickly defeated by Prussian troops. Schurz fled from Germany, knowing the Prussians would execute him if they caught him. But when he learned one of his favorite professors had been imprisoned, he sneaked back into Germany and organized a prison break to free his friend.

After briefly living in England and France, Schurz immigrated to the United States in 1852. He bought a farm in Wisconsin and immediately became interested in American politics. Morally opposed to slavery, Schurz was attracted to the Republican Party because of its anti-slavery stance. He began campaigning for Republican candidates, giving speeches in both German and English. Even before he became a U.S. citizen, Schurz ran unsuccessfully for lieutenant governor.

During the Civil War (1861-1865), Schurz joined the Union army. He also became a close friend and adviser to President Abraham Lincoln. After the war, President Andrew Johnson asked Schurz to tour the South and report on conditions there. Schurz's influential report recommended that free slaves be given the right to vote. Schurz spent the next few years writing for several newspapers, including a German language daily.

Remaining active in Republican politics, Schurz was elected to the U.S. Senate in 1869. Eight years later, following an unsuccessful re-election bid, President Rutherford B. Hayes appointed him secretary of the interior. In that post, Schurz worked to improve the government's treatment of American Indians.

Schurz returned to journalism in the 1880s. He served as an editor at the *New York Evening Post* and an editorial writer for *Harper's Weekly*. Through his writing, Schurz continually celebrated American-style democracy. He repeatedly reminded his readers that immigrants like himself were often "more jealously patriotic Americans than many natives are." Since his death in 1906, history has remembered Schurz as a skilled politician, a gifted orator, and, above all, a passionate patriot.

their present. He hailed them as a people who had retained their connection to their old country even while establishing loyalty to a new fatherland. But, despite the German Americans' enthusiastic embrace of the United States, this loyalty would soon be questioned as America entered two wars with Germany in the first half of the twentieth century.

When Schurz spoke to fairgoers in St. Louis, the great wave of German immigration to the United States had recently come to an end. Immediately after Bismarck united Germany, the number of German immigrants had briefly risen. Many of the new immigrants were German Catholics, who wanted to escape oppression under Bismarck's rule. In an attempt to unite the German people culturally as well as politically, Bismarck had initiated the *Kulturkampf* (culture struggle)—a set of policies and laws that encouraged Germans to embrace Protestant religions and abandon the Roman Catholic Church.

But quickly the immigration trend reversed. The successful economic policies of Bismarck convinced many Germans who may have been inclined to emigrate in the past to stay in their newly unified homeland. As Germany became even more prosperous, fewer Germans saw immigrating to the United States as their only means of bettering themselves financially. They could now find work and make a decent living in their own country.

Even as immigration slowed, German Americans still made up a large percentage of the American population. At the beginning of the twentieth century, they numbered approximately 18 million. About one of every four Americans had German ancestry.

GERMAN-AMERICAN ALLIANCE

To look after their interests, the German-American Alliance was founded in 1901. Within 15 years, its membership grew to 3 million, making it the largest organization representing an ethnic group in the United States. The alliance dedicated itself to preserving German-American culture. Among its missions were promoting the use of the German language, opposing limits on immigration, and funding monuments commemorating German-American heroes, including a statue of Germantown's founder, Francis Daniel Pastorius.

Another important goal of the Alliance was to fight Prohibition, a movement to outlaw the consumption and manufacture of alcohol. The Alliance was heavily funded by wealthy German-American brewers, who would be put out of business if the Prohibitionists had their way. But above wanting to protect these businessmen, the Alliance viewed the Prohibition movement as essentially anti-German. In one publication, the Alliance branded Prohibition as an attack on "German manners and customs, the joviality of the German people." The article concluded, "in order to gain for the Germans of America that place in the sun which has hitherto always been denied them, it is absolutely necessary that they enjoy personal liberty, and that this shall not be whittled away by the attacks of the prohibitionists and the persecutors of the foreign born."

By 1914, the German-American Alliance was engulfed in battling a new threat to its membership—the possibility that the United States would go to war with Germany. In that year, the conflict that later became known as World War I broke out in Europe. The war pitted Germany against England, France, and Russia.

Most German Americans wanted the United States to stay out of the World War I. But much of the American press had a pro-English bias and called for the nation to enter the conflict. To counter press reports that painted Germany in a negative light, the German-American Alliance began publishing a magazine titled *The Fatherland* in 1914. The Alliance also organized mass demonstrations in support of American neutrality and took up collections to help German victims of the war. Other German-American clubs and churches joined the effort to provide war relief. They raised millions of dollars to feed starving German children.

The German-American Alliance also took an active role in trying to defeat Woodrow Wilson's bid for the U.S. presidency in 1916. Although Wilson promised to keep the United States out of World War I, he had a decidedly pro-British stance. During his election campaign, Wilson displayed contempt for German Americans who expressed sympathy for their former homeland. In one speech, he declared, "I am the candidate of a party, but I am above all things an American citizen. I neither seek the favor nor fear the displeasure of that small alien element which puts loyalty to any foreign power before loyalty to the United States." Despite the Alliance's best efforts, Wilson won the presidency.

AMERICA ENTERS WORLD WAR I AGAINST GERMANY

In April 1917, Wilson ended American neutrality by joining the war on the side of the Allied forces, which included Britain, France, and Belgium, to name a few. With the United States at war with Germany, German-American clubs and newspapers scrambled to declare their loyalty to the United States. Many organizations counseled their members, for their own safety, to keep any pro-German sentiments they might have to themselves.

In fact, many German Americans were unsure of how they felt about the conflict. Considering themselves both American and German, they found it difficult in their hearts to wholly support either side. German-American writer Hermann Hagedorn described his own mixed emotions on hearing news from the war front: "Soberly gratified though I might be at every German setback, every German victory set my Teutonic [Germanic] heart beating a little faster. Ambivalence is the word for it . . . it made for tension and a feeling of guilt."

ANTI-GERMAN SENTIMENT

The rest of the American public, however, was united in their hatred for the German enemy. The entire country was swept up in a wave of anti-German sentiment. To display their patriotism,

The events of World War I tested the loyalty of German Americans to their new homeland of the United States, and the tolerance of non-German Americans to accept these German-American immigrants as "true" Americans. The German-American Alliance unsuccessfully opposed the election of Woodrow Wilson for president of the United States, because of Wilson's stance against German Americans who expressed sympathy for their homeland.

Americans burned German books, banned the performance of music by German composers, and renamed towns and streets that had long been known by German names. Even favorite foods from Germany were renamed to remove their association with the enemy. Suddenly, Americans were eating hot dogs instead of frankfurters and liberty cabbage instead of sauerkraut.

Much of the anti-German hysteria was directed against the German language. Expressing the views of many Americans caught up in the frenzy, a state legislator in Nebraska declared, "If these people [German Americans] are Americans let them speak our language." Many states forbade or restricted the teaching of German. In a few, speaking German in public was outlawed. Out of fear, many German-American churches began holding services in English. German-American newspapers were censored and, unable to attract advertisers, many went out of business.

Average German Americans also came under suspicion. Wild rumors spread of their supposed acts of sabotage on the American home front. Friends and neighbors shared false stories of how German Americans were trying to destroy American morale. In Ohio, German-American meatpackers were accused of putting glass in sausages, while in Colorado, German Americans working for the Red Cross were said to have infected bandages with bacteria. The Ohio militia was even sent out to protect the state's water supply from being poisoned by German saboteurs.

HARASSMENT AND ATTACKS
AGAINST GERMAN AMERICANS

To root out German spies and sympathizers, the Justice Department organized the American Protective League, a group made up of 200,000 untrained volunteers. The league never found a single German spy, but it did succeed in harassing hundreds of innocent Americans of German ancestry. Its volunteers contributed to an atmosphere of suspicion that grew nearly unbearable for many German immigrants. German-American Helen Wagner described the miserable conditions in Yorkville, a German-American neighborhood of New York City, during the war:

> Those war years were really pathetic. You couldn't walk the street with a German paper under your arm. You'd be abused from one end of the block to the other. They went so far they abused the poor little German dogs that walked the street. That's the hatred that was. We kept speaking German at home, but we avoided it on the street.

Vigilante groups added to the terror felt by German Americans who tried to hide their ancestry for fear that their houses and businesses would be vandalized or burned. German Americans unlucky enough to be branded as disloyal also had to fear for their physical well-being. Vigilantes often humiliated suspected German sympathizers by marching them through the street and forcing them to recite the Pledge of Allegiance or sing the U.S. national anthem. If their victims resisted, they were beaten.

Some German Americans lost their lives at the hands of angry mobs. One was Robert P. Prager, a coal miner living in Collinsville, Illinois. As the police looked on, vigilantes seized Prager and publicly lynched him on April 5, 1918. His murderers later stood trial, but all were acquitted.

To escape a similar fate, German Americans made dramatic displays of patriotism. They spent millions on Liberty Bonds, which the U.S. government sold to help fund the war effort. They held parades and rallies to declare their love of America and the American way of life. Many German-American men showed their loyalty by joining the military. Among them were a large number of war heroes, including General John J. Pershing and Captain Eddie Rickenbacker.

CONSCIENTIOUS OBJECTORS

Generally, German Americans offered little resistance to being drafted into the U.S. military services. Exceptions were Mennonites and Hutterites, whose religion forbade them from engaging in violent acts. These German Americans became conscientious objectors, refusing to join the army on religious grounds. Most were jailed in federal prisons, where they were treated harshly. Two Hutterite men imprisoned in South Dakota died of pneumonia after being exposed to harsh winter weather. Thereafter, the Hutterite leaders began sending young men in their communities to Canada to save them from the draft.

As America entered World War I, anti-German sentiments in the United States ran high, and sometimes resulted in outright acts of violence against German Americans. Some German Americans, like American flying ace Eddie Rickenbacker, escaped this fate by distinguishing themselves in battle as members of America's armed forces.

POST-WAR DECLINE OF GERMAN CULTURE IN AMERICA

World War I ended in 1918 with Germany's defeat. The worst of the wartime oppression of German Americans came to an end, although the memory of what they suffered remained strong. Many German Americans—especially those born in the United States—gave up trying to preserve their own culture. They had learned what a high price they might pay for drawing attention to their German heritage. Settled and content with their lives in the United States, they preferred to be seen not as German Americans, but just plain Americans.

The anti-German fervor of the war era had also taken a

great toll on nearly all German-American institutions. The German-American press was devastated. By the end of the war, about half of German-American newspapers operating in 1917 were forced to close. Many German clubs and organizations as well disbanded during the war, never to be formed again.

One of the greatest losses for the German-American community was the dissolution of the German-American Alliance. In early 1918, the U.S. Senate held hearings to determine whether the Alliance was a threat to the American war effort. The hearings cast a shadow over the organization, convincing the public that the Alliance was somehow un-American. Its leader, Siegmund von Bosse, received so many death threats that he had to go into hiding. In July 1918, Congress revoked the Alliance's charter, but by that time, the organization had already disbanded. After the war, the Steuben Society was founded as a national organization to defend the rights of German Americans. But with a membership of only about 20,000, it never wielded near the power that the Alliance had before World War I.

PROHIBITION'S EFFECT ON BREWERIES

German-American culture was dealt another blow with the passage of the Volstead Act of 1919, which made Prohibition the law of the land. Prohibition forced the family-oriented German beer gardens to close, thus putting an end to a treasured part of German-American life. Several German-American breweries also went out of business. Their closure in turn brought an end to many German-American organizations, which relied on the financial support of wealthy brewers. German-American journalist H. L. Mencken wrote bitterly of the victory enjoyed by Anglo-American Prohibition advocates in imposing their values on German-American society: "They lust to inflict inconvenience, discomfort, and, whenever possible, disgrace upon the persons they hate—which is to say, upon everyone who is having a better time in the world than they are."

WORLD WAR II AND HITLER'S EFFECT ON GERMAN AMERICANS

In the early 1930s, German Americans faced another crisis when Adolf Hitler became the dictator of Germany. (Hitler and his followers, known as the Nazis, began enforcing oppressive laws, especially against Germany's Jewish population, and voicing a desire to invade other European nations.) With Hitler's rise to power, German Americans feared that, once again, they would become the targets of a renewed anti-German movement. German immigrant Werner Cottbus later recalled how the attitudes of his schoolmates changed toward his brother and him as news of Hitler's atrocities spread:

> [W]e got along rather well, or as well as you could, being German kids in the Bronx [a borough of New York City] between the two wars. They'd call us names: "Hey Germany!" and all that. Then, as we got into 1933, 1934, it became the Hitler and Nazi thing. Our high school in the Bronx was mainly Jewish, and it got to be rather difficult with both teachers and students.

In 1939, Hitler sent German troops into Poland. As a result, England, France, and several other nations declared war against Germany. With their suffering during World War I fresh in their minds, most German Americans wanted the United States to stay out of the new European conflict, which became known as World War II. Their feelings were well-expressed by an article in December 1939 in *Youth Outlook German-American Monthly,* a magazine published by the German-American League for Culture: "It is our interest that America not be led once more into fighting the battles of Europe, for Hitler's oppressive rule can only be abolished by the oppressed themselves. We support the fight of the German people for their liberation and we regard it as our duty to preserve the real German culture and the traditional democracy of the United States."

Despite the strong opposition to Hitler in the German-American community, some Nazis still sought support from Germans in the United States. As early as 1924, the Nazis tried to recruit German Americans to their cause with little success. In 1933, Hitler's supporters attempted to form a pro-Nazi organization in the United States called the Friends of New Germany. The organization fell apart after being investigated by Congress, but was soon succeeded by the *Deutschamerikanische Volksbund* (German American People's League), more popularly known as the *Bund*.

THE BUND

Organized by Fritz Julius Kuhn in 1936, the Bund claimed to have 200,000 members at its height. In fact, it probably never had a membership of more than 6,500. Most Bund members were young men who had recently emigrated from Germany. Many were laborers who were having trouble finding work during the Great Depression of the 1930s. Anxious about their future, they found comfort and fellowship by participating in Bund meetings, often during which members marched with wooden guns to military music. Many participants were more attracted to the Bund's pageantry than its politics. For instance, Alfred Krakau, a member of the *Deutsches Jugendschaft* (German-American Youth Movement), a youth organization associated with the Bund, explained, "I liked the music and the marching, all that bombastic stuff that youth seems to like."

The Bund came to the attention of the American public after holding two huge rallies at New York City's Madison Square Garden in 1936 and 1939. Each event drew a crowd of more than 20,000. The majority of attendees, however, had little interest in actually joining the Bund. Some came out of curiosity, whereas many others were lured to the rally by its organizers' offer of free beer.

Although the Bund had almost no substantial support in the United States, Congress began investigating the group in

1938. Reminiscent of the German-American Alliance hearings, the investigators harassed and insulted German-American witnesses, with little regard to whether or not they were Bund supporters. Amid the negative publicity associated with the hearings, the Bund fell apart. It disbanded completely after Kuhn was imprisoned for embezzling Bund funds in 1939.

During the Bund's years of operation, its influence had been negligible. Only a tiny fraction of German Americans had any sympathy for the organization. Nevertheless, the Bund's activities reignited suspicions about the loyalties of German Americans.

OPPOSITION OF GERMAN AMERICANS TO HITLER'S TACTICS

In fact, as German Americans heard more and more tales of horror about life under the Nazi regime, they overwhelmingly came to support the defeat of Hitler. When the United States entered World War II in December 1941, most German Americans enthusiastically supported the decision. Many German-American men enlisted to join the fight. Up to one-third of all American military personnel during the war were of German ancestry. The commander-in-chief of the armies of the United States and its allies—Dwight D. Eisenhower—was a German American.

SOME GERMAN AMERICANS SENT TO INTERNMENT CAMPS

Even with their enthusiasm for the war against Hitler, German Americans were sometimes accused of siding with the enemy. Stories of German-American spies were spread in many sensationalist articles and books. Eager to sell their work, writers made wild claims about widespread German-American disloyalty. One such author was F. W. Foerster, who wrote in his *Open Letter to the Loyal Americans of German Descent* (1943) that "many German-Americans have been willing, even ardent collaborators in this vicious Pan-German plot."

As Hitler rose to power in Germany in the 1930s, German Americans again became victims of prejudice. Anti-German feeling in America erupted for the second time in three decades.

Despite these efforts to fan the flames of anti-Germanism, most German Americans were spared from the oppression and violence they had experienced during World War I, largely because of their vocal opposition to Hitler. However, about 11,000 German Americans fell victim to the FBI's efforts to detain people it identified as dangerous to the American war effort. These German Americans were taken from their homes and sent to more than 50 internment camps throughout the United States. There, many spent years living within barbed wired fences, watched by armed guards.

Some of the German-American internees had been members of the Bund. But others had never shown any public support or sympathy for the Nazis. Many were sent to the camps after being turned into the FBI by friends and neighbors for the most minor of offenses. Belonging to a German-American organization or attending a German Day celebration was enough to make a German American vulnerable to internment. In violation of the U.S. Constitution, German-American internees were denied legal counsel and were not allowed to face their accusers. Although the federal government's internment policy affected a relatively small portion of the German-American population, it succeeded in sending a message to all German Americans: merely by mentioning their ethnic background in public, they would be placing their freedom at risk.

EMIGRATION CONTINUES

Despite this oppression, the United States was the destination of choice of many emigrants who fled Germany during the war. Between 1933 and 1945, about 130,000 Germans and German-speaking Austrians fled to America. Many were Jews, who were the targets of systemic murder by the Nazi regime. For many German émigrés, their arrival in the United States was bittersweet. While they celebrated their liberation from the Nazis, they mourned the devastation of Germany and the suffering of its people. In her journal, Hertha Nathorff, a German refugee who escaped to New York City in early 1940, wrote of the horror she had left behind as she celebrated Christmas in her new homeland:

> None of us wants to speak about our life back there. We know how much it would hurt, and today is Christmas, a holiday. We took a walk through Central Park. It is glorious in its winter splendor, and all the happy, laughing people on our way made my heart lighter. Perhaps one day we too will stroll through Central Park happy and laughing, sit quietly on a bench late in the evening and enjoy the sea of lights, the blinking lights of the skyscrapers all around us, and our hearts won't cringe in pain as they did today.

7

INTO THE MELTING POT:
The German-American Influence

It is no easy task to summarize the manifold influences German-Americans have exerted on American society and culture, as they are so diverse and deeply interwoven into the very fabric of American life. . . . If you scratch the surface of something in America, the chances are high that a German origin is underneath. . . . What is American is often German-American in origin.

— The German-American Experience **(2000)**
by German-American scholar Don Heinrich Tolzmann

The trauma of the two world wars deeply affected German-American society. By 1945, when World War II ended with the defeat of Germany and its allies, many German-American institutions had long disappeared. Clubs and organizations had

Among the German Jews who fled Hitler's Nazi regime were many noted scientists and intellectuals, perhaps the most famous being physicist Albert Einstein, whose theories reshaped the way we view space and time.

disbanded, newspapers had gone out of business, and schools had closed their doors for good. Further demoralizing to German Americans was the devastation of the old country. Years of warfare left Germany not only in ruins, but politically divided. During the post-wars years, Germany was split into two separate nations—West Germany, a democracy, and East Germany, a Communist nation.

DISAPPEARANCE OF GERMAN-AMERICAN CULTURE

Daunted by their treatment during the early twentieth century, most German Americans had given up drawing attention to their ethnic background. Recent immigrants, many of whom were Jews who felt lucky to escape from Hitler's Germany alive, were even more reluctant to bring up their heritage. Unlike some earlier German immigrants, they had no romantic illusions about the old country. They were eager to forget about the fatherland altogether and settle into their new lives as Americans. As a result, by the late twentieth century, German-American culture seemed to have disappeared completely from American society. However, beneath the surface, the German influence on economic, social, and cultural life in the United States remained surprisingly strong.

GERMAN CONTRIBUTIONS TO AMERICAN LIFE

Agriculture

One of the many fields in which German Americans made enormous contributions was agriculture. Largely because of the labor of German Americans, the farms established in the midwestern states helped feed the nation throughout the nineteenth and twentieth centuries. Still today, German Americans dominate American agriculture. More than one-third of American farmers are of German ancestry. In 12 states in the Midwest, nearly half of the farming population is German American.

Business and Electrical Engineering

German Americans were also instrumental in the evolution of American business and technology. Throughout the nineteenth century, German tradespeople and artisans crafted many of the goods—from shoes to furniture to books—used by all Americans. Educated in the excellent engineering schools of their native country, Germans helped establish many new industries in the United States. One such innovator was Charles P. Steinmetz, the founder of General Electric, a company that revolutionized the field of electrical engineering. Working in a lab in upstate New York, Steinmetz was nick-named the Wizard of Schenectady, an honor he earned by inventing more than 100 electrical devices. Another outstand-ing German-American engineer was Johann A. Roebling. Roebling was an expert bridge-builder. His masterpiece was the Brooklyn Bridge, which connects the boroughs of Brooklyn and Manhattan in New York City.

Science

Especially during the World War II era, German Americans came to dominate American science. Among the best-known were German-American scientist J. Robert Oppenheimer, who led the team of physicists that invented the nuclear bomb, and Albert Einstein, who made great contributions to modern physics with his theories of relativity. At the center of the U.S. space program were scores of German scientists who left Germany in the 1930s and 1940s to escape the Nazis.

Since the United States' beginnings, it has relied on German Americans for its military strength. German-American soldiers have played a substantial role in every war in which the United States has engaged, beginning with the American Revolution. During the nineteenth and twentieth centuries, they made up about one-third of the country's military forces.

Music

German Americans have been equally influential in the development of the arts in the United States. Given the German people's love of music, it is hardly surprising that many conductors, opera singers, and music teachers in the United States are of German heritage. The music-loving German Americans as well helped popularize in America the work of German composers, such as Wolfgang Mozart and

Ludwig von Beethoven. People of German ancestry have also written many of the greatest patriotic songs in American music. John Philip Sousa wrote marches such as *Stars and Stripes Forever,* while Georg Drumm composed *Hail to the Chief,* the song often traditionally played when the president of the United States enters a room. Also of German ancestry was bandleader Lawrence Welk, whose musical variety show was one of the most popular programs in early television history. Welk's show featured old-fashioned songs he had played at German-American wedding parties early in his career.

Literature

Another passion of the German people, reading, accounts for the large number of German-American writers. American novelists of German descent include Theodore Dreiser, Gertrude Stein, John Steinbeck, and Kurt Vonnegut. Thomas Mann, one of Germany's greatest writers, immigrated during the war, became a U.S. citizen, and wrote some of his finest work in America. German Americans have also made their mark in children's literature. Among them are two of the most beloved children's writers of all time—L. Frank Baum, author of *The Wizard of Oz,* and Theodor S. Geisel, better known as Dr. Seuss.

Art

The visual arts as well owe a debt to German Americans. Some of the most stirring paintings of the American landscape were made by nineteenth-century German immigrant Albert Bierstadt. In the early twentieth century, the German-born Alfred Stieglitz became known as the "father of American photography." Many German painters who fled Europe directly before and during the World War II era—including Josef Albers, Max Ernst, Hans Hofmann, Ad Reinhardt, and Franz Kline—helped make the United States the center of the art world in the last half of the twentieth century. During the same period, German immigrants Walter Gropius

Notable German Americans

John Peter Zenger (1697–1746) Born in Germany, Zenger moved to New York City at 13. After eight years as a printer's apprentice, Zenger established a printing house in 1726. A year after his newspaper, the *New York Weekly Journal,* published articles attacking New York's colonial governor William Cosby in 1733, Zenger was arrested for libel. Zenger was brought to trial after a 10-month imprisonment. His trial resulted in an acquittal, and the landmark court case established the principle of freedom of the press in colonial America.

John Jacob Astor (1763–1848) The son of a butcher, John Jacob Astor was born near Heidelberg, Germany. Twenty-one and penniless, he immigrated to the United States in 1783. Astor entered into the fur trade and through his American Fur Company he soon amassed an enormous personal fortune. A series of shrewd investments in New York City real estate made Astor the richest man in America at the time of his death.

Thomas Nast (1840–1902) Born in Landau, Germany, Nast moved with his family to New York City when he was six. After Nast worked as an artist for several New York newspapers, he joined the staff of *Harper's Weekly* as a cartoonist. His best-known cartoons ridiculed New York mayor William Marcy Tweed and Tammany Hall, Tweed's corrupt political machine. In early 1902, President Theodore Roosevelt appointed Nast consul general of Guayaquil, Ecuador, where Nast died on December 7.

Franz Boas (1858–1942) As a boy in Minden, Germany, Franz Boas developed a keen interest in science. After moving to the United States in 1887, he became editor of *Science* magazine. Boas later taught anthropology at Columbia University where his students included the famous anthropologists Margaret Mead and Ruth Benedict. Boas lived among several native North American peoples, including the Inuits and the Kwakiutls. The founder of the American Anthropological Association and the author of many classic books, Boas is now considered the father of American anthropology.

Albert Einstein (1879–1955) Einstein was born in Ulm, Germany. Although a poor student, he showed a keen interest in mathematics and science. After attending college in Switzerland, Einstein worked in a Swiss patent office and wrote scientific papers in his spare time. His theories revolutionized the field of physics and earned him a Nobel prize in 1921. Fleeing Nazi Germany, Einstein immigrated to the United States in 1933. During World War II, he helped convince President Franklin D. Roosevelt to establish the Manhattan Project, which led to the development of the atomic bomb. Einstein spent his final years at a post with Princeton University's Institute for Advanced Study.

Notable German Americans (continued)

Dwight D. Eisenhower (1890–1969) The first president with a German name, Eisenhower was the supreme commander of the Allied Forces during World War II. He supervised the Allies' successful invasion of Europe in June 1944. In 1952, Eisenhower ran for president on the Republican ticket. President Eisenhower worked to end the Korean War and prevent the spread of Communism. He served two terms before leaving the White House in 1961. Eisenhower died of heart failure in 1969.

George Herman "Babe" Ruth (1895–1948) Ruth was born in Baltimore, where he began his professional baseball career in the minor leagues. In 1914, Ruth was sold to the Boston Red Sox as a pitcher. Six years later, he joined the New York Yankees, for whom he played outfield. Ruth's many records include the highest lifetime total of homeruns (714)—a record that stood until Hank Aaron broke it in 1974. Ruth played in 10 World Series before retiring in 1935 and was one of the first five players elected to the Baseball Hall of Fame in 1936.

Marlene Dietrich (1901–1992) Born in Berlin, Germany, Dietrich became an international sensation when she appeared as Lola-Lola, a captivating night-club singer, in *Der Blaue Engel* (The Blue Angel) in 1930. She then moved to the United States, where she became one of Hollywood's greatest stars. Denouncing the politics of German chancellor Adolf Hitler, Dietrich became a U.S. citizen in 1937. During World War II, she performed in more than 500 shows for American troops and their allies.

John Steinbeck (1902–1970) Born in Salinas, California, Steinbeck was a day laborer while beginning his writing career. He had early success with *Tortilla Flat* (1935) and *Of Mice and Men* (1937) before publishing *The Grapes of Wrath* (1939), which won the Pulitzer Prize and was made into a classic film. His later works include *The Pearl* (1948), *The Red Pony* (1949), *East of Eden* (1952), and *The Winter of Our Discontent* (1961). Steinbeck was awarded the Nobel Prize for Literature in 1962.

Maria Goeppert Mayer (1906–1972) Born in Kattowitz, Germany, Maria Goeppert earned a PhD in physics at the University of Göttingen. After marrying American scientist Joseph E. Mayer, she moved to the United States, becoming a U.S. citizen in 1933. Mayer, whose research focused on nuclear physics, developed a theory that the nucleus of an atom consists of several shells made up of protons and neutrons. Working with German physicist J. Hans D. Jensen, she wrote *Elementary Theory of Nuclear Shell Structure* (1955). Mayer and Jensen won a Nobel Prize in 1963 for their pioneering work.

and Ludwig Mies van der Rohe steered the course of American architecture by pioneering the construction of glass-covered skyscrapers. The art of cartooning has also been greatly influenced by German Americans. In the nineteenth century, Thomas Nast was regarded as America's greatest political cartoonist, whereas in the twentieth century, Charles Schulz created Charlie Brown, Snoopy, and many other beloved characters in his newspaper strip *Peanuts*.

Education

Perhaps the field in which German Americans have had the greatest influence is education. The very structure of American education is largely based on educational philosophies developed in Germany and introduced to the United States by German immigrants. The idea of kindergarten (German for "children's garden") was brought to America by intellectuals who left Germany after the failed revolution of 1848. Physical education in American public schools was advocated by German immigrants influenced by the Turner movement, which taught that a sound mind and a sound body go hand in hand. Other German educational reforms adopted in the United States included vocational education and cooperative on-the-job training for high school students.

German Americans were also pioneers in bilingual education. The first bilingual public school program—which included classes taught in German and English—was founded in 1840 in Cincinnati, Ohio. In many other states with large German-American populations, similar programs were started at the demand of area voters.

Hard Work and Play

The enormous achievements of German Americans bare witness to their dedication to hard work and diligence. This characteristic is undoubtedly one of their greatest contributions to American culture, as it helped to create a strong work ethic that continues to drive the U.S. economy. But perhaps equally as important is the spirit of frivolity Germans interjected into the American way of life. In the eyes of German immigrants, Americans of English ancestry often placed too much emphasis on the difficulties of human life and not enough on its pleasures. One German woman who immigrated in the early nineteenth century said of her Anglo-American neighbors, "They do not love music; and they never amuse themselves; and their hearts are not warm, at least they seem so to strangers; and they have no ease, no forgetfulness of business and of care, no not for a moment." To German immigrants, relaxing with friends and family was a central part of life. One of the personal qualities they most valued they called *gemütlichkeit*. It was used to describe a person who was joyful and easygoing, even in the face of adversity.

Christmas Celebration

With these values, it is not surprising that German immigrants have had a huge influence over the way Americans celebrate holidays. Almost every aspect of the American Christmas celebration draws on German traditions. In 1821, German settlers in Lancaster, Pennsylvania, erected the first Christmas tree in the United States. Their Anglo-American neighbors were disturbed by the display, suspecting that somehow it was ungodly. Nevertheless, by the next decade, other Americans began imitating the German custom of bringing an evergreen inside and decorating it with candles, fruits, and ornaments. Use of this Christmas decoration became more widespread after news reports described the beautiful tree displayed in the Boston home of Karl Follen, the first professor of German to teach in America.

German Christmas customs were further popularized by the publication of *Kriss Kringle's Christmas Tree* in 1845. (Kris Kringle was a version of *Christkindl*, the German word for the

Much of the way Americans celebrate Christmas owes its origin to German customs. The German character, *Saint Nicholas*, became known in America as *Sinterklaas,* and later Santa Claus. The jolly bearded figure in the red suit who we recognize today was, in part, the creation of Thomas Nast, the German-born cartoonist at *Harper's Weekly* magazine.

Christ child.) German traditions included giving toys to children on Christmas. Among the Pennsylvania Germans, the gifts were often distributed by men wearing fake beards and bishop hats. They were dressed to resemble St. Nicholas, whom the

Pennsylvania Germans called *Sinterklaas*. German-American cartoonist Thomas Nast drew illustrations of this figure with a long white beard and a fat belly, creating the character we know as Santa Claus.

Easter

German immigrants also introduced many of the rituals Americans now associate with Easter. As Germans did in Europe, they celebrated the end of Lent by eating colored eggs. Traditionally, German parents secretly placed the eggs in nests built by their children, leaving them believe the eggs were laid there by what Germans called the Easter hare. Gilbert J. Jordan described how he celebrated Easter as a child in a German-American community in Texas:

> On the Saturday before Easter we children always went on a flower-hunting expedition. We took a child's wagon and some baskets or buckets and went out to the pasture and fields to gather flowers and fresh grass for our Easter nests. We fixed the nests on the front porch, where the Easter rabbit could easily find them. . . . Naturally we children never had any part in the egg dyeing; this was the Easter rabbit's job.

Food

Part of every German celebration was feasting. As a result, the wonderful culinary traditions of Germany were another important contribution immigrants made to American life. Among the foods introduced to the United States by Germans were pretzels, apple streudel, sauerkraut, potato salad, and mustard. Germans also gave Americans two of their favorite foods—frankfurters and hamburgers—both of which were named after German cities. Beer was still another German gift to American cuisine. Many of the major brands of American beer—from Schlitz to Pabst to Budweiser—still bear German names.

Many common American foods originated in Germany. Pretzels, potato salad, frankfurters, and sauerkraut all got their start in German kitchens.

FESTIVALS AND PARADES

The traditions of German-American celebrations live on today in the hundreds of Oktoberfests held throughout the country. Usually held in October, these events re-create the atmosphere of the old German beer gardens, where people gathered to eat, drink beer, and listen to music. Among the largest Oktoberfests are those held in Cincinnati, Ohio, and LaCrosse, Wisconsin—both cities with especially high concentrations of German Americans. Each November, the old German settlement of New Braunfels, Texas, also hosts a Wurstfest. Hundreds of thousands of people attend the festival to enjoy a meal of bratwurst or other traditional German sausages. Ironically, the old German customs preserved at these celebrations are now almost unknown in Germany. As writer Susan Stern has noted, "[I]f you want to see traditional German costumes, feast on sausages and sauerkraut, sway arm in arm at a beer table—you might have an easier time in Indianapolis than in [the German cities of] Berlin or Düsseldorf."

German Americans also come together at annual parades held in New York, Philadelphia, Chicago, and other major American cities. Many are held on German-American Day—October 3, the date Germantown, Pennsylvania, was founded. Other parades are staged on Steuben Day (September 17) to commemorate the birthday of Friedrich Wilhelm von Steuben, the greatest German-American hero of the American Revolution.

RECENT CELEBRATIONS

Along with these annual celebrations, two recent events have helped foster a new sense of group identity among German Americans. In 1983, millions joined in celebrating the Tricentennial of the founding of Germantown. Thousands of museum exhibits, conferences, concerts, parades, and other events were held to commemorate the event. The U.S. government marked the Tricentennial by issuing a commemorative stamp and donating land near the Washington Monument for the German-American Friendship Garden.

The second event occurred on German-American Day in 1990. After the collapse of the Communist government of East Germany, East and West Germany were consolidated into one country. More than a century before, German Americans celebrated the unification of the German states. In a similar fashion, the reunification of Germany in the late twentieth century gave Germans in the United States a renewed feeling of pride in seeing Germany once again poised to take its place as one of Europe's largest and most powerful nations. As one German newspaper explained in 1992, "German unification triggered a wave of sympathy in the USA and fostered a new self-awareness among German Americans."

PRESERVATION OF GERMAN CULTURE TODAY

Although German club life declined after the two world wars, several associations remain committed to promoting German-American culture. The Steuben Society, based in New York City, continues to draw a national membership. Founded in Chicago in 1958, the German-American National Congress (also known as DANK) has also emerged as the leading voice of German-American communities in the Midwest.

The once vibrant German-American press has nearly disappeared, though a few newspapers have survived. Most notable is the *New Yorker Staats-Zeitung*, which has been published for more than 150 years. More recently, *German Life* magazine was founded to offer information on German-American history and on sites and events of interest to German Americans today.

Also eager to preserve German-American culture are several notable archives and museums. The Society of German-American Studies was founded in 1968. In addition to publishing the *Journal of German-American Studies*, it has set guidelines for teaching German-American studies on the university level and initiated the campaign for federal recognition of German-American Day. In New Braunfels, Texas, people interested in German-American history can visit the Sophienburg Museum, which houses hundreds of artifacts from the town's earliest days. Another facility of note is the Schifferstadt Architectural Museum, located in Frederick, Maryland. It includes the restored

German architecture has also exerted its influence on American design. In addition to many tourist villages and parks, many town buildings (like this post office in New Ulm, Minnesota) still bear the mark of their German heritage.

house of Joseph Brunner, a German who immigrated to the United States in 1744.

To attract tourists, several American towns have been redesigned to resemble old villages in the German state of Bavaria. These tourist attractions include Frankenmuth, Michigan, and Leavenworth, Washington. Somewhat more authentic is MainStrasse in the historically German-American town of Covington, Kentucky. This area features five blocks of restored eighteenth- and nineteenth-century structures, including the Mutter-Gottes-Kirche (Mother of God Church), which was constructed by German Catholics in 1842.

American visitors to these attractions come to experience a piece of German-American history and heritage. But, in fact, they could do that without leaving home. Owing to the great contributions of Germans to the United States, the influences of German Americans run deep through American life, helping to give it its unique shape and flavor. That these influences are hardly discernible now is a testament to the German-Americans' ability to thrive in their new land. Perhaps more than any other American ethnic group, they succeeded both in bringing the best of their homeland to America and in incorporating the best of America in themselves.

C. A.D. 1000	Tryker the German is a member of Leif Ericsson's expedition to Vinland.
1608	Several Germans move to the English settlement of Jamestown, Virginia.
1618–1648	The Thirty Years' War destroys much of the German population and countryside.
1683	The first German settlement in America is founded in Germantown, Pennsylvania.
1735	Printer John Peter Zenger is acquitted of libel charges, thus establishing the tradition of freedom of the press in the American colonies.
1775–1783	All-German regiments battle for American independence.
1778	Prussian military officer Friedrich Wilhelm von Steuben becomes the inspector general of the American army.
1806	Napoleon defeats and dissolves the Holy Roman Empire of the German Nation.
1821	The German Christmas tree is introduced to America by Germans in Lancaster, Pennsylvania.
1829	Gottfried Duden publishes a travel book about living in America, prompting thousands of Germans to emigrate.
1848	Political radicals stage an unsuccessful revolution in Germany.
1849	German revolutionaries, known as the Forty-Eighters, escape to the United States.
1856	Margaretha Meyer Schurz establishes the first kindergarten in America in Watertown, Wisconsin.
1862	The Homestead Act offers Americans free western land, further inspiring German emigration.
1870	Otto von Bismarck unifies the German states.
1872	Thousands of German farmers flee Russia to avoid military service; many immigrate to the United States.
1873	Bismarck launches the *Kulturkampf*, driving many German Catholics to leave for the United States.
1882	More than 250,000 Germans come to America, making 1882 the greatest year of German immigration.
1886	The Haymaker Riot in Chicago prompts the execution of August Spies, editor of the *Arbeiter Zeitung*.
1901	The German-American Alliance is established.

1917	The United States enters World War I; Americans respond with hostility toward German Americans and their culture.
1920	Prohibition is instituted, destroying the businesses of German-American brewers.
1923	The Supreme Court rules unconstitutional the prohibition on teaching the German language in American schools.
1933	Adolf Hitler becomes chancellor of Germany; German scholars and artists begin arriving in the United States to escape the Nazi regime.
1941–1945	The United States enters World War II as Germany's enemy; 10,000 German Americans are confined to internment camps.
1968	The Society for German-American Studies is founded.
1983	The Tricentennial of the founding of Germantown, Pennsylvania, is commemorated.
1987	The U.S. government officially recognizes October 3 as German-American Day.
1989	German-American Heritage Month is established.
1990	German Americans celebrate the unification of Germany.

Anderson, Mark M., ed. *Hitler's Exiles: Personal Stories of the Flight from Nazi Germany to America.* New York: New Press, 1998.

Conzen, Kathleen Neils. "Germans." *Harvard Encyclopedia of American Ethnic Groups,* edited by Stephan Thernstrom. Cambridge, MA: Belknap Press, 1980.

Gottfried Duden, *Report on a Journey to the Western States of North America and a Stay of Several Years Along the Missouri (During the Years 1824, '25, '26, and 1827).* Edited by James W. Goodrich. Translated by George H. Kellner, Adolph E. Schroeder, and Wayne Senner. Columbia, Missouri: State Historical Society of Missouri, 1980.

Fox, Stephen. *America's Invisible Gulag: A Biography of German American Internment and Exclusion in World War II.* New York: Peter Lang, 2000.

Flynt, Josiah. "The German and the German-American," *The Atlantic Monthly* 78 (November): 469, 1896.

Hoobler, Dorothy and Thomas. *The German American Family Album.* New York: Oxford University Press, 1996.

Kamphoefner, Walter D. et al, eds. *News From the Land of Freedom: German Immigrants Write Home.* Ithaca, NY: Cornell University Press.

Luebke, Frederick C. *Germans in the New World: Essays in the History of Immigration.* Urbana: University of Illinois Press, 1990.

McCormick, E. Allen, ed. *Germans in America: Aspects of German-American Relations in the Nineteenth Century.* New York: Brooklyn College Press, 1983.

Rippley, La Vern J. *The German-Americans.* Boston: Twayne Publishers, 1976.

Rippley, La Vern J. "German Americans." *Gale Encyclopedia of Multicultural America,* edited by Judy Galens, Anna J. Sheets, and Robyn W. Young. Detroit: Gale Research, 1995.

Tolzmann, Don Heinrich. *The German-American Experience.* Albany, NY: Humanity Books, 2000.

FICTION

Gündisch, Karin. *How I Became an American.* Chicago: Cricket Books, 2001.

Levitin, Sonia. *Silver Days.* New York: Atheneum, 1989.

Rinaldi, Ann. *Keep Smiling Through.* San Diego: Harcourt Brace, 1996.

NONFICTION

Franck, Irene M. *German-American Heritage.* New York: Facts On File, 1988.

Hoobler, Dorothy and Thomas. *The German American Family Album.* New York: Oxford University Press, 1998.

Shnidman, Ellen. *The German-American Answer Book.* Philadelphia: Chelsea House, 1998.

American Family Immigration History Center at Ellis Island
http://www.ellisisland.org

German Life Magazine
http://www.germanlife.com

The Germans in America
http://lcweb.loc.gov/rr/european/imde/germany.html

Immigration History Research Center at the University of Minnesota
http://www1.umn.edu/ihrc

Max Kade Institute for German American Studies
http://csumc.wisc.edu:16080/mki/

Pennsylvania Dutch Country Welcome Center
http://www.padutch.com

German American National Congress
Executive Offices, D.A.N.K. Haus
4740 N. Western Avenue
Chicago, IL 60625

German Society of Pennsylvania
611 Spring Garden Street
Philadelphia, PA 19123

Pennsylvania German Cultural Heritage Center
P.O. Box 306
Kutztown University
Kutztown, PA 19530

Society for German-American Studies
German Department
St. Olaf's College
Northfield, MN 55057

Steuben Society of America
6705 Fresh Pond Road
Ridgewood, NY 11385

page:

13: © Kelly-Mooney Photography/Corbis
17: Fred Hultstrang History in Picture Collections, NDIRS-NDSU
18: National Archives at College Park, College Park, MD
21: © Adam Woolfitt/Corbis
24: Hierophant Collection
27: American Memory: Photographs of the Detroit Publishing Company
31: © Bettmann/Corbis
35: © Peter Harholdt/Corbis
39: Hierophant Collection
44: © Christie's Images/Corbis
46: © Corbis
49: Fred Hultstrand History in Pictures Collection, MDORS-NDSU, Fargo
50: © Minnesota Historical Society/Corbis

53: © Corbis
63: © Bettmann/Corbis
66: Hierophant Collection
71: Hierophant Collection
73: © Corbis
74: © Bettman/Corbis
82: ©Hulton-Archive/Getty Images
85: National Archives at College Park, College Park, MD
90: National Archives at College Park, College Park, MD
93: AP/National Museum of History & Technology
101: ©Hulton-Archive/Getty Images
103: © Dave Bartruff/Corbis
106: National Archives at College Park, College Park, MDs

Cover: © Pat O'Hara/Corbis

Frontis: Courtesy University of Texas at Austin, Perry-Castañeda Map Collection, CIA map.

LIZ SONNEBORN is a writer and an editor, living in Brooklyn, New York. A graduate of Swarthmore College, she has written more than 25 books for children and adults, including *The American West*, *A to Z of American Women in the Performing Arts*, and *The New York Public Library's Amazing Native American History*, winner of a 2000 Parent's Choice Award.

DANIEL PATRICK MOYNIHAN is a former United States senator from New York. He is also the only person in American history to have served in the cabinets or subcabinets of four successive presidents—Kennedy, Johnson, Nixon, and Ford. Formerly a professor of government at Harvard University, he has written and edited many books.